FROM DEATH TO LIFE

A TRUE STORY OF MIRACLES

RACHEL BENSON

LIFEWISE BOOKS

FROM DEATH TO LIFE
A TRUE STORY OF MIRACLES
BY RACHEL BENSON

Published by:

 LIFEWISE BOOKS

PO BOX 1072
Pinehurst, TX 77362
LifeWiseBooks.com

Interior Layout and Design | Yvonne Parks | PearCreative.ca

To contact the author:
www.RachelBenson.com

ISBN (Print): 978-1-947279-13-1
ISBN (Ebook): 978-1-947279-14-8

DEDICATION

Jesus – Thank you. Without you,
none of this would be possible.

Mom and Dad – You both have been there for me
throughout my entire life. Without your constant and
consistent support, life would have been a lot different.
I love you.

Friends and Mentors – My heart is filled with an ocean of
gratitude for the truly amazing people in my life.

TABLE OF CONTENTS

INTRODUCTION

Welcome to my journey—my journey of hope. Hope became real and tangible with the experiences I share here. This book is a story of what miracles God can do with a girl who had no faith, hope, or belief that He existed, from gut-wrenching experiences of pain, hurt, and trauma to real life-changing encounters with our living God. It has been a blessed journey without an end. My life story so far includes many miracles as God began building me into His image, from before I knew God existed to the present.

In my ignorant years, I walked contrary to God's ways, from my youth to when I was diagnosed with multiple sclerosis. This has been a personal journey of healing, hope and truth. Thank you for walking through the pages with me as I share how God revealed himself to me. I will take you through some of my darkest hours to bring you into the light, which only God could have led me to. I pray that my testimony imparts hope and healing to you. Let the journey begin.

CHAPTER 1

HE WAS ALWAYS WITH ME

FEAR WAS EVER PRESENT

Growing up, I was terrified of the dark. On occasion, I would see dark shadowy figures moving around my room and house that filled me with fear. Peace was mostly absent from my childhood, especially when it was time for bed. For much of my younger years, when it was bed time, I would lie awake for what felt like an eternity. Day dreaming, or visions while awake, happened often. This was my normal. I remember looking at the world as a little girl and wondering if I was all alone on earth.

These scary dreams and experiences isolated me in my mind and feelings from a very young age. I had no idea these dreams were far from normal. I don't have any memories of talking about what was happening to me with family or friends. Fear was a big part of my life. It plagued my thoughts and mind constantly, from my first and few childhood memories.

My mind was dominated by thoughts that I was on my own in this area of my life. A stage was being set for me to believe lies. No one else I knew dealt with the nightmares and scary experiences I was having. Growing up in a nice neighborhood on Long Island, New York, I had many good times and lots of fun with family and friends. The incredible summers at the beach and sailing with my dad were some of my most memorable moments.

My family created a good environment for exploring what I loved to do and finding tangible success. My life was filled with lots of friends and so many fun, creative, new things to do. Yet fear was always lurking, and the nightmares were constant. Later, I found out that God was there for me before I knew Him. This truth has brought me to a place of gratitude that far surpasses any known comprehension. I have said this to a few people along the road of my life: "…if every tormenting and terrifying experience only brought me closer to God, it was all worth it."

Please, join me, as I invite you on my journey. It is a tale of my life from before I knew our God existed until now. Now, I not only know he exists, I know he loves us and is with us with our every breath. No matter what we're facing, God is greater than anything the world tries to throw at us.

A GIFT REVEALED

A gift of discernment was placed inside me. The revelation of this comes from my one of my earliest memories. Having a sense of people, their motives and intentions, was something I had heightened awareness of from a very young age. At the time, there was no explanation for this. I was told as I was growing up that "it's intuition, it's your gut, it's your "knower." Oddly, I was usually right on with what I was sensing about a person. I don't recall any mention of God or that it was a gift from God.

My mom shared her love of horses with me growing up. That was wonderful. We would go to the horse stables and ride western style. Gradually, my mom's love of horses led her to buy her own horse. My mom worked diligently in her career, and this was a true joy for her. Saddles, boots, and most items for the horse world are expensive. One lady befriended my mom at the stables. I never felt comfortable around her. I can recall being uneasy around her on-site. I had no idea what I was sensing.

My mom and dad called me the "people tester" when I was a kid. As it turns out, this lady stole some expensive horse tack from my mom. I remember wondering in my single digit years, why can't everyone see this? It was so clear to me not to trust her. It was a gift given to me by God, which I would find out later: the gift of discernment.

BORN JEWISH – A BLESSING

Growing up and being born into a Jewish home was a blessing, although, I had no idea who God was yet. I didn't go to Hebrew School, and I don't recall why. My rebellion may have had something to do with it. I don't remember any talk of what the Jewish religion meant. Although I am sure it was discussed, my childhood memories are very few.

My brother went to Hebrew school and had his bar mitzvah. That was quite the party, but I don't remember the Jewish temple experience for the bar mitzvah, which was his coming of age. There were so many family and friends celebrating my brother. I was nine years old and remember it being a wonderful celebration. From my perspective while growing up, being Jewish was more of a culture in our home. An acknowledgement and appreciation of being Jewish and celebrating the Jewish holidays was always present.

IN MY DREAMS

My parents gave me a stable home and environment. They always wanted the best for me and did everything they could do to provide just that. Yes, this was a blessing, but I had to know more about what I was dealing with, from the nightmares and the dark figures I would see sometimes at night to feeling people's emotional and sometimes physical hurts. I had no idea how or why this was happening and what it meant. It terrified me and left me with so many questions. Confusion was something not new to me as little girl. This all led me to search for answers from a very young age.

My first memories of these experiences go back to when I was five years old. It may have started before that age, but my memory doesn't allow anything prior to that age right now. Memories are few from my childhood, but I can remember running from the hallway of my parent's home to leap into my bed. I was terrified that the creatures I dreamed about and sometimes saw from the corner of my eye during waking hours would grab my legs and pull me down with them. That never happened, but the fear of it happening was real enough that my imagination would run with it, and fear would only build.

Sometimes I saw the dark figures in the waking hours too, not just my sleep time. They usually looked like a greyish-black figure, a silhouette. As soon as I landed in my bed, I would lie there and stare at the ceiling for what seemed like an eternity before I fell asleep. My bedroom wasn't what I consider now a safe zone. It was the place where the quiet at night left me terrified of what fear would lie about next. By the time I was in elementary school, I had many friends and was a rather gregarious and playful child. Life seemed to be going well, minus the hell I went through at night and the glimpses of the darkness I saw and felt during my waking hours.

THE POWER AND PRAYER

It was blessing to see God's hand in my life. Let's fast forward, thirty years into the future. The power and effectiveness of prayer were revealed. One night when I was in my mid-thirties, I had a friend request on Facebook. She was someone I went to high school with. We proceeded to have a nice conversation on my Facebook wall. That's when she mentioned that it was hard for her in elementary school. One reason was because I was so mean to her. I sat there in my home feeling so sorry for hurting her, repenting and asking for forgiveness from her and God. She was so happy I was a Christian now.

She shared how her mom told her to pray for me. When she would go home and tell her mom how mean I was to her, her mom would say, "You don't know what she's dealing with, just pray for her." I remember sitting there starring at my computer and just sobbing. I thought, "Dear Lord, you are amazing. You had someone praying for me during the scariest times of my life before I knew you." Not just someone, but another little girl whom I had hurt. I have learned this much—hurting people can hurt others. Her mom was wise and loving, and I am eternally grateful for them and their prayers. Although I had no idea what the prayer or the power of prayer meant yet, God knew what I needed. He provided for me before I even knew he existed.

THE MISSION TO FIND ANSWERS

These scary experiences were part of my formative years, and I accepted them as normal. As I approached the age of accountability, I was led on the search for the meaning of life and God everywhere. It seems like a rather young age to have such passion for these explanations. My self-proclaimed mission was to find answers for the terrifying and unexplainable things happening to me. The experiences I had with the supernatural in my early years were mostly accompanied by fear and torment. That will all change in the years to come.

My sleep time and sometimes waking hours were greatly affected. This journey to find answers to my many questions, led me down many mislead roads over my formative years and into my 20's. This is when I dove into occult practices. By high school, full immersion in these practices was made manifest. I had many experiences with the supernatural as a child. My dream life was bombarded with what I know now as demonic activity. Before this truth was revealed, I just thought these scary creatures that would torment me at night in the horrible dreams were normal. Fear was my normal.

A lot of my younger years were filled with unrestful sleep and what you can call nightmares. On one occasion, I awoke to a creature hovering over me, pinning me to my bed. I screamed, but no audible sounds would come out. Fear led me into more isolation. After a what seemed like hours, which was in reality only seconds, it would go, and I would get up and start my day. It was as if the prison of fear I lived in was something only I could see and experience. On occasion, I saw the dark shadows moving around my bed, my room, and other areas of the house. Were they ghosts? That's what I believed at this point, although I learned later what they really were. When this would happen, I would go about my day trying to block it all out. I believe I tried to share what was going on with my family. I interpreted their responses as that they didn't understand. It's not they didn't care. They loved me and wanted the absolute best for me. I can only assume, they thought it was my creative mind at work. These traumatic experiences were becoming my norm.

There was constant unrest in my soul, which consists of the mind, will, and emotions. I had no idea why I was so tormented by these horrible creatures. It didn't make sense. I remember jumping at playful banter between family and friends, and at loud noises. It was as if I was being stalked by an unseen scary force.

At this point in my life, now in my teen years, I knew intimately about fear and torment. It's important to reiterate, I came from a good family and no harm was done to me by my parents or brother. We had typical disagreements and quarrels that you could expect in any household, like my parents sending me to my room when I didn't do my chores or talked back to them. I know it sounds rough, but I actually came from a great family. My family just didn't offer any explanations to all these questions as to what was happening to me. How could they? Up until this point, no one I knew talked about what I was experiencing. I kept it mostly to myself. I thought, I must be the only one experiencing this.

I was so young when this all started. I felt very alone because of these scary experiences. The absolute lie that I was alone in this world was formed from a very young age. That's when the journey down the wrong road began. I was introduced to New Age book stores to find the answers. I figured they would know. I had no affiliation with the synagogue. I had never read the Torah and was basically Jewish by birth and not yet meaning. I figured The New Age talked about this kind of stuff, right?

Some of their books talked about scary experiences I was having. From what I can recall, the books I read didn't mention anything about demons. At the New Age book store, I received more questions than answers. I had no idea what I was about to invite into my life. Unknowingly, I had invited hell into my life. This was a time in my life where I received countless psychic readings for over seven years. I was searching for the answers as to what was happening to me.

Psychics claim to talk to spirits that can provide information pertaining to your life, past, present, and future. These people seemed to understand what I was experiencing and provided explanations, which were mostly lies. The search made me even more hungry for truth, for answers. Nothing was satisfying my hunger for the truth. At this point, my thirst was unquenched. Every time I saw a psychic, they would say I had the same gift they had. As a teenager, that sounded so alluring and wonderful. They always got very excited when sharing with me about my life, which I thought they were hearing from a good source. Interestingly, the psychic readings never filled a place in my soul or heart. I can recall always feeling a sense of emptiness after I left their presence.

This made me want more of what they offered. The desire and thirst only grew. I know it now as seduction, designed to build me up and expect great things—which is wonderful, but the great things to expect had no mention of God or Jesus. It intrigued me, and it was slowly seducing me to walk their way. This led to a more in-depth investigation into the occult. I now know it's not a psychic gift I have, but a gift of prophecy as stated in the Bible: "Your sons and daughters will prophesy."[1]

Psychics don't work with The Holy Spirit. Anything shared contrary to God's Spirit and Word is a counterfeit. The Bible is clear; it's called divination. God's word is clear about divination, and there are many scriptures pertaining to the matter. This one in particular speaks directly to the deception of psychics and or medium: "Do not defile yourselves by turning to mediums or to those who consult the spirits of the dead. I am the Lord your God."[2] Most of the people I encountered involved in new-age were very nice and truly wanted to help. I learned later on that It wasn't the person's intention to deceive me, it was the enemy of our soul deceiving me. They most likely didn't know they were being used by a source that wasn't God.

DECEPTION LED ME DOWN THE WRONG ROAD

I had no idea I was defiling myself. This was the beginning of unconsciously and unknowingly walking in deception. I was desperate for answers, and I read every book I could get my hands on that dealt with, ghosts, channeling spirits, UFOs, angels, witchcraft, you name it and more. UFO books were something I threw myself into, too. I needed to know what was going on. I had what I thought were encounters with these strange "alien beings." I had no idea what was happening. This wasn't something you talked about in my nice, middle-class American family.

One afternoon I was taking a nap in my parent's bed at eighteen years old. They had a big, comfy bed and the best comforter. In the dream, two tall, very skinny creatures with big black eyes came floating quickly towards me down the hallway. All the while they were talking to me with their minds. I was pinned to the bed and screamed "NO, NO, NO," in my mind, "you can't take me again!" The fear overtook every part of me.

I woke up sweating and crying. I knew inside every part of me something had interrupted them from taking me. They weren't good creatures, and I don't believe they were what people call aliens today, coming from another planet to research us or help us humans out. It's my belief these beings were far from benevolent. They left me with the same feelings of horror I had during the demonic nightmares.

This wasn't anything I felt I could talk about with anyone. I mean, really? There was no way I was going talk about the scary dreams with my friends from high school and college. That wasn't the life I led or wanted to lead, so I just blocked it out the best I could and dealt with it on my own. Yet, I was and still am so investigative, which led me to seek answers at the New Age bookstores. Oh yeah, there were a lot of answers. The answers I found there were mostly based on lies, to be discovered years later.

This was when I began practicing the occult. I mentioned seduction, and this was all part of being seduced by the wrong team leading me down the wrong road. I read Tarot cards for myself and others, and that opened more doors to the wrong road. Why do I call it the wrong road? Anything contrary to God's word is a deception. So much of what I was about to embark upon was completely contrary to his word.

I started working with the ouija board (talking to what I thought was the dead) and casting spells, otherwise known as witchcraft. I remember feeling a sense of what I know now as false confidence and false empowerment. When I was experiencing it, I thought it was real. It wasn't until I started to walk in the true reality that this all started to make some sense. Jesus is the way—he is the truth and life. The proverbial lights would be turned on soon enough.

GLIMMERS OF HOPE

Before I knew him, God was there with me the whole time. My heart was to truly know the truth. I believe God knew this about me because He actually knows all my thoughts. He never stopped pursuing me. The enemy of our soul comes to steal, kill, and destroy us. I didn't know any of this truth yet, but our loving God was with me through it all. He is greater than anything the enemy says or does. The enemy has already been defeated. I was to learn all of this in years to come, and hope was right around the corner.

These experiences continued to propel me into the occult to find answers. Although I was Jewish, I had not been to Hebrew school and didn't seek any answers from my Jewish faith. Some of my friends were Catholic, and that intrigued me. When a few friends of mine talked about God, I saw a light in some of their eyes. That excited every part of me. My first known encounter with God's presence was quite notable. When I was in high school, I went to a friend's Catholic church. It was not for a service—she had to stop there to get something and I went in with her. A feeling of safety invaded every part of me, perhaps for the first time ever. This memory stays with me.

What I know now as God's presence was there, and I had the sense all was going to be okay. I cried that night, desperately wanting more of this. I knew in my gut that the presence of God I experienced is what I needed.

It wouldn't be for several years that I would meet Jesus face to face. He was all I needed and didn't know it yet. I learned later, the enemy of our soul disguises himself as an angel of light.[3] It wasn't just tormenting, scary experiences and dreams I had with the enemy of our soul. I'd had many deceiving experiences too. Why would a person trust, welcome, or accept a presence as good that is so scary? I was unknowingly traveling down a road of self-deception. I had come to think I was powerful when I knew stuff before it would happen.

Actually, reading people's thoughts sometimes happened too. I could feel people's feelings. When I was nineteen, my first boyfriend and I were on the beach, and I remember answering his questions. I can recall a blank stare as he fixed his eyes on me in with bewilderment. He said, "I didn't say anything, I was thinking those things!" I sat there, and I can distinctly recall feeling a sense of bewilderment, wonder, and power. I had no idea what was operating at the time. I know now, it was actually a spirit in me operating and not a good one. I had no idea, and it wouldn't be discovered until years later. All of this was about me, what I was doing, and what power I could access to have control. I call them pride-puffers, among other things that are not very positive. I was being groomed for the enemy's camp and didn't know it. It would be a few years before this truth all started to unfold.

I have since encountered and learned that God is so much greater than what the father of lies says or does. I learned later, God was with me through every terrifying moment. Not only was he with me, I would learn that he is greater than the scary creatures. God has intervened in my life in ways I am barely aware of. The word of God says, "I knew you before you were formed in your mother's womb.[4] God was always with me before I knew he existed, before I knew he was there with every breath I would take. He was with me through all the times I was terrified and didn't know if I was going to make it to the next day. My goodness, our God formed us in our mother's womb. He loved us before we would even take our first breath.

Most of my younger years were filled with fear and terror. God's love is something I had yet to fully experience. Good times were had too—I was an active kid and was living a seemingly normal, middle-class American life. If there was anything that required running, jumping, and swimming, that was for me. So many dreams were nurtured. During these wonderful times, the experiences I had in the unseen led me to so much despair, torment, and confusion. I felt all alone in the world, and by the time I was in college, the intensity of what I was dealing with as a kid had gone to new levels. Thoughts of giving up on life had invaded.

MASQUERADE

Torment was my norm most of my younger life. Another unwelcome encounter occurred. A nap on a couch in my parent's home in the middle of the day was most welcomed during my busy college class schedule. Suddenly, I was standing at the foot of the first-floor staircase. When I looked down I saw my legs hovering above the stairs. I perceived that I was not in my body. Then in an instant, I felt like I was being sucked up the stairs at the speed of light. I was then moved to the next landing, where the second floor met the third- floor staircase.

Cries echoed out of me, "no, no, no!" The words, "You can't take me" came screaming out of me. I had no idea why I was saying what I said or who I was talking to. All I knew was it wasn't' a good place I was being taken to, and the one taking me wasn't good. During the perceived out-of-body experience, I screamed from every part of me, "Let me go!" When I arrived at the second-floor landing, I stood there facing what looked like a portal to another world and screamed for my life for help. That's when I was immediately slammed back into my body, and I came up out of the experience. To this day, I don't know how to explain what happened. All I remember vaguely is the terror I felt in the experience. What I like to believe is that our loving God intervened and helped me back into my body. This all happened before I invited Jesus into my heart and was one of the reasons my search led me down the wrong roads.

GOD WAS ALWAYS THERE

When we are saved, His Spirit lives in us forever. We are literally born again. That means the enemy of our soul cannot do the things he used to do--simply put, his status is "ACCESS DENIED," to our spirit. These experiences were terrifying and made me believe the lies, yet they were exciting at the same time. Seduction to the wrong road is appealing to the flesh and the soul. The truth had yet to be revealed. The deceptive road I was traveling on seemed real. In actuality, it was being built on lies. Yet, God was always there through it all.

I had friends most of my life who knew Jesus. Sometimes a friend's parents or a friend would say to me that they're praying for me. That always sparked a sense of wonder, yet it was a foreign concept back then. The memories from my early years are very sparse. I have since learned that is indicative of trauma. I can't recall the nuggets spoken to impart hope and life, but I know it was shared.

From fear to substance abuse, my norms were mostly negative by the time I entered college. Experimenting with illegal substances and drinking alcohol excessively to escape was now a new norm. By this time, I was practicing spells on a regular basis and had embraced this deceptive path. A lying perception of myself had invaded, and my life was not based on any truth yet. It was as if a cape of false confidence had been placed over me to cover up the fear that was with me. I was having many supernatural experiences. They didn't breathe the breath of God yet. What was to come via supernatural experiences would blow every terrifying experience I ever had out of the water. Our God was about to reveal who He is to me personally.

ENDNOTES

1. Acts 2:17
2. Leviticus 11:19
3. 2 Corinthians 11:14
4. Jeremiah 1:5

CHAPTER 2

NEVER THE SAME

ISOLATION AND BELIEVING LIES

The more tormenting experiences with the scary creatures I had, the more I hid inside myself. Isolation was something I knew very well. I chose to isolate myself in my thoughts, figuring no one understood me. I was an outgoing kid who loved sports, fun, friends, and adventures. There was freedom to dream in my home. I would dream of traveling around the world at a very young age, helping people, becoming a veterinarian and so many other wonderful things that were a seemingly normal existence. Yet, I always had this lurking, dark world with me. I had yet to fully experience God's goodness, his love, his grace, and his peace.

There were fleeting moments of peace, although the constant and pervasive reality I knew was fear. Simply walking up the stairs to watch TV in my parent's home had to be planned on most occasions. I remember going up the stairs very quietly, looking intently with anticipation of seeing the scary creature on or around the couch. It was the dark shadow of a person I saw. I only saw it there a few times, but the terror of it being just around the corner was always with me. I know now I was seeing a demonic spirit.

Demons are evil fallen angels who follow Satan instead of God. Later I learn that as a born-again believer, I have all power and authority over these demons, in Jesus' name. A great example of this truth is found in Luke 10:19, "Look, I have given you authority over all the power of the enemy, and you can walk among snakes and scorpions and crush them. Nothing will injure you."

Fear had been so built up in me that all I knew how to do was to survive each moment. I was a little kid trying to make sense of a perceived scary world. My perception was not real. It was formed by fear. I don't know how I started thinking that those creatures were going to harm me. I would soon learn that the enemy of our soul is the father of lies. An acronym for fear that is so very true is "false evidence appearing real." Basically, lies putting on a show and are based in no reality. What the enemy meant for harm, God uses for His good. I am living proof of this and am blessed to live this out today.

ENDING IT ALL

My first memory of wanting to take my own life was at the age of five. I was on the playground and I recall having the thought, "how can I escape this scary world?" I didn't want to be here, yet I didn't know about heaven or hell yet. The desire to not want to be here on earth stayed with me through my developmental years and into my young adult years. The nightmares were so traumatic, I would wake up not wanting to be here anymore. I have pondered this for some time now. Why on earth does a five-year-old want to die? Especially a kid who has good parents and every need and most wants provided for.

Over the years, I have received wise and most helpful counsel. One thing I did was seek out healing for my soul. I chose to ask Holy Spirit to go to the places in my soul and heal any wounds there. For example, I commanded all trauma to leave, in Jesus' name. It was more extensive than that, but suffice it to say I sought healing and deliverance by most credible and wonderful people in ministry and counseling. This part of my journey is a possible future book.

If you're thinking of hurting yourself, I am by no means an expert in counseling and I am not a licensed counselor. I am not qualified to offer any professional advice, but my heart is to share my story to impart hope. If you're having thoughts of harming yourself, my suggestion is to please seek help from credible and qualified professionals. I am happy to say the issue of wanting to take my own life has been dealt with for several years now. Praise God, I have been set free from what was tormenting me and any desire to want to harm myself has been eradicated. I live a life that speaks of freedom today.

NEW HEIGHTS OF TERROR

The scary and tormenting dreams started to intensify the closer I got to the experience that would change me forever. At twenty years old, I was living on the beach with a friend in Ocean City, Maryland, one summer. It would be almost seven months before I moved out to Arizona to finish college. One summer night, I was sleeping by myself at our little rented shack on the beach. I lovingly called, paradise. It was then I awoke in terror with what I thought was a man on top of me.

When I tried to scream, nothing came out. When I tried to rip him off me, I couldn't grab any part of his body. There was no form to him, yet the terror of his hurting me was there. It was as if it could touch me and

I couldn't touch it. I use the word "it" on purpose. Suddenly, I realized it was one of the scary creatures. I knew them well, and this one was trying to have its way with me. I don't know how it happened, but I do remember it just suddenly disappeared and was unable to hurt me or violate me.

If memory serves me correctly, my dear friend who was in the bedroom next to me prayed for me. She'd had a near-death experience a couple months prior, and she knew Jesus intimately due to her supernatural experience. I thank God for her and her prayers. Prayers are so powerful, and they can move mountains. I believe God interceded that night and subsequently the creature was unable to hurt me.

I then went outside right after the almost traumatic occurrence and sat on our porch to catch my breath. It was late and oddly quiet that night. We lived in party central. Most nights were filled with lots of college-aged kids carousing, drinking alcohol, and being loud right outside my little shack on the beach. This night, all was still. The terror from what had just happened was present. Looking up at the sky, I distinctly remember saying out loud and clearly, "God if you're real, I need help and I need it now." Desperation for help was at a new level.

AN ENCOUNTER WITH GOD'S KID

Our next-door neighbor pulled into his driveway adjacent to me. He looked at me as he was walking into his little beach house. Not two minutes later he came back outside and walked over to me in an unobtrusive manner. Now, I hadn't met him or his roommate yet. The summer was nearing the end, and I had only seen them come and go. They didn't party, drink, or anything else. Apparently, they were there to make money for their college education. As it turns out, they were nice Catholic boys.

He came over and asked me, "Are you ok? God wanted me to come and talk to you." No one has ever said these words to me before. I sat there pinned to my chair. I thought, "God are you real? Did you hear me crying out to you just now?" Tears started to flood my face, and I shared how a scary creature tried to hurt me. That's when he began to tell me how his father traveled the country praying for people with the exact problem I was having. He mentioned Jesus, exorcisms, and to be honest, that freaked me out. It was a term I had only heard of in scary movies. The movie *The Exorcist* came to mind. Deliverance is what I needed; I just didn't know it yet. After this young man left my porch and went inside, I knew now God was the only one who could help me. Hope was something I tasted for maybe the first time.

THE ENEMY'S ATTEMPT TO RECRUIT ME

Upon my return home from the beach in Maryland, life sped up rather quickly. God was moving, and I had yet to recognize that as such. One of my first trips was to a local New Age store on Long Island. I frequented it often, searching for answers to what was happening to me. The intensity of the scary experiences was magnified now, to a new degree. So, I went to where I was comfortable to search for the answers. It was getting harder to hide under any veil of denial. This is where I met a man who was the partial owner of the New Age bookstore. We had a connection, so I thought, and then he sent me a rather lovely poem in the mail. We then started to date.

In retrospect, I recognize this now as the enemy of my soul trying to recruit me to his side. The man was a self-professed warlock, or a male witch. I was twenty years old and had my whole life awaiting me. We entered into a relationship rather quickly. He shared a lot of what he walked in with me. That led me deeper down the rabbit hole, and my understanding and practice of witchcraft went deeper.

Then one night, he asked me to marry him. I was shocked and said, "No, I can't marry you, I am still in college and need to finish my degrees." That was what I was raised to do, or so I thought. I know it now as God working in me to keep me safe, and I had no idea yet. The no took him by surprise, and he ended the relationship a few days later. I gasp now at how God took care of me. The thought of being married to a warlock is unfathomable now.

DREAMS IN THE NIGHT
THAT WOULD COME TO PASS

Shortly after the relationship ended with the man from the new age book store, I Suddenly started having dreams during my sleeping time of Arizona. I knew I needed to get there. It had been my heart's desire to move to Arizona for some time. The lobbying started; I pitched the idea of finishing college in Arizona to my parents, and they lovingly agreed. Their support was so very generous, they paid my whole way to Arizona and everything else. Right before I left Arizona, I was having what I know now as prophetic dreams. In one very vivid dream, I dreamt of the man I had yet to meet who would ultimately lead me to my encounter with Jesus. I would find out soon that he lived in Arizona.

I can still remember another dream I had only days later as if it just happened. I dreamt of two Rachel's. One Rachel (me) had long hair and was standing in the sun with the most brilliant light all around me. My eyes were shinning with so much love. The other Rachel (me) was in a couture business suit. I was anorexic thin, and my eyes had no life in them. I remember waking up and gasping for air. This was all around the time I was trying to decide whether to come to Arizona or not. I had this incredible sense that if I stayed in NY, the Rachel who had no life in her eyes is what I would have become; if I went to Arizona, the Rachel with life and joy is what I would become. I do believe I made the right choice. A few months later, it all happened so quickly. It was a no brainer. I was now in Arizona, my soon-to be home. Now, I can reflect on that dream and identify with the Rachel filled with life. The other Rachel does not exist.

AN ENCOUNTER WITH JESUS

The silent years of torment and fear culminated in a life-changing encounter one night. I was leaving New York with expectation for only the best and embracing Arizona as my new home. Then it happened; I had only been here for a few months. My dark and dismal story was about to take a directional change that breathed life into my immortal soul forever. It all led up to a night when my life was changed for eternity. The memory of this night's experience is as clear as if it happened just yesterday.

This night started out so very dark and void of any hope. My whole intention in moving to Arizona was to finish college and begin the next exciting chapter of my life. I didn't just move my body across the country. I moved my thoughts, my heart, my spirit, and my dreams, and every tormenting thought and spirit came with me too. The nightmares had increased, too, and sleeping was traumatic almost every night now. Growing up, I had several nights without the tormenting dreams; now it was almost constant.

One evening, I spent most of the day crying in my bed at my studio apartment. I remember lying in my bed with no vision of anything good. I felt like I was being suffocated. There I was, twenty-one and wanting to end my life. I had purchased a gun, and it rested on my bed, a small sigma 380. I pondered and wrestled with myself, wondering if I could even kill myself successfully. Up to this point in my life, I felt like a miserable failure, which was just one of the negative lies I believed. I couldn't take the torment anymore not one more nightmare.

That's when my phone rang. I answered it, and it was a new friend on the phone. It was the friend I dreamt about in NY before I moved to Arizona. I don't recall what I said verbatim. I do know I told him I wanted to die, and I couldn't take it anymore. I can't recall if I had shared about the nightmares yet with him, yet. He had convinced me to give him a key to my apartment a few weeks prior. If memory serves me correctly, his reasoning was, "You're out here all alone, and it's wise to give a key to someone, just in case anything happens." I found out later, he was a Christian, and Holy Spirit must have told him to get a key to my apartment because I was suicidal.

I was crying the ugly cry with him on the phone that night. Suddenly, I looked up from my bed and saw the front door to my apartment open. It was surreal, and in my conscious mind, I had no idea what was happening. I was taken by surprise. He then he walked in with a friend of his. This was before the days when you assume everyone is on a cell phone, so in my mind, he was still across town. He and his friend had been sober for several years and were in AA. I learned later that my call was indicative of a twelve-step call.

They entered rather quickly, and his friend took the gun off my bed and left. It seemed like it happened in a flash. My new friend looked at me and said, "Rachel, you most likely would have ended up in hell tonight had you gone through with this." I recall sitting there visibly shaking. It was the most real moment of my life up until that moment. I just knew in my knower that he was right. Never before had I heard truth that echoed through every part of me.

I had yet to understand the "why." Why would I have ended up in hell had I taken my life that night. I was about to discover the only way to Father God is through, Jesus. I didn't know Jesus and hadn't received him as my Lord and savior yet. My friend then then showed me a scar that went from his wrist all the way up his arm. As he pointed to the scar on his arm, he continued to tell me about an experience when he almost died and how God brought him back. The experience he shared with me included an encounter with Father God, Jesus, heaven and an almost encounter with hell. He shared how hell was real. He also shared how God and Jesus were real and more powerful, then the scary creatures. This life-giving information was all brand new to me.

I told my friend that the nightmares were getting worse, and I couldn't take it anymore. The thought of heaven was so new, and I wanted to know more. Then he said something no one else had ever said to me. He said, "You can take Jesus into your dreams." I believe that's when a glimmer of hope was birthed in me. I had heard of Jesus before, but never like this. He talked about him as if he was real and his best friend. This was a night when I was sober, and I hadn't had any alcohol in my body all day. I was exhausted from crying most of the day and into the night. It was time to rest, so I laid down to go to sleep. That's when my life changed for eternity.

You may have heard of Muslims in war-torn countries having encounters with Jesus in their dream time and awakening with a full revelation that he is not only real, but the son of God. I was about to have a similar experience. With my eyes closed, I soon went to into a deep sleep. That's when I went into the dream where the "monsters" would come for me—a dream I had for years and years in various forms of torment.

In this instance, I recall a seven-foot disfigured and gruesome male type figure with a 13th-century cape standing in right front of me. I could feel its breath on my face. It was a scenario I knew well. I then looked at its eyes, and it morphed, suddenly looking like my friend who came to my house that night. Instantly, I knew it wasn't my friend; the eyes were dark, terrifying and soulless. I then exclaimed loudly, "I know who you are—you're not my friend!" The creature then morphed back into a hideous monster. There were ancient tablets/scrolls with words in a foreign language inscribed on them in the sky above me. The scrolls and tablets cracked open in the sky, and it was dark outside in the dream. There was an ancient language of some kind being written in the sky. The creatures always had a flair for the dramatic; they liked the attention to be all about them and to instill fear.

In sheer desperation, I cried out for the first time ever, "Jesus help me!" The moment I cried out to Jesus, the horrible creature was sucked away from me. The creature was turned into what looked like a little black fly. I know that now as the truth. They were never that big and scary. They only portray themselves this way to instill fear and a false sense of power. Again, the enemy is the father of lies. That was a lie I had believed up until that very moment. My surroundings completely changed in the dream. I was now surrounded by light, and the love I felt was like nothing I had known before.

Jesus was with me, and I knew it was him. It was as if I had known him forever. I was in the presence of love. A love I had not known before that moment. The love, peace, and security I experienced were filled with life so brand new to me. I was experiencing now what I know as the living truth, Jesus. It would be a few years until I learned more of what that meant. I was in the presence of the Son of God. I was about to learn and discover what this word means. "Jesus told him, 'I am the way, the truth, and the life. No one can come to the Father except through me.'"[1]

Upon awakening from my forever-changed encounter with Jesus, I woke up to what I know now as the Holy Spirit filling my whole apartment. My apartment was filled with a notable and tangible, peaceful atmosphere that remained for a several minutes. The quiet peace and love I felt in the dream were now translated into my waking hours. Tears of relief streamed down my face, with a relief I had not known before my encounter with Jesus. This was just the beginning. Not only did I have a life-changing encounter with our savior Jesus Christ, but the memories of the demonic nightmares were completely erased that night, never to return in memory or dream again. Thank you, Jesus, for this miraculous gift.

MUCH, MUCH MORE TO COME

It has been almost twenty-two years since my first encounter with Jesus. Yes, I said first encounter. The second face to face encounter with Jesus happened eleven years later. That encounter was an invitation that will be shared in the pages to come. Since the first encounter, I have never had another night terror like the ones that plagued me up until the night I encountered Jesus. God delivered me from the nightmares. I have had unpleasant dreams, but not ones that include the torment from what I know now as demons. This life-changing encounter with Jesus rearranged my life. All my ideas, values, thoughts, dreams, and basically everything started to change. It wasn't all about me anymore. A new life had just started. The pursuit of him had just begun.

ENDNOTES

1. John 14:6

CHAPTER 3

THE SEARCH FOR THE TRUTH

LIFE JUST TOOK ANOTHER TURN

Gratitude was defined the night of my life-changing encounter with Jesus. You would think after my encounter with Jesus that I would have ended up in a church, pursuing who he was in the Bible with other believers. Who was Jesus—this was my burning question? The answers had yet to be explored. Here I was, twenty-one years old with my whole life ahead of me and still hurting in my soul. I had yet to know this, but healing and deliverance were needed from a lifetime of trauma I experienced in the unseen world and not living right. Freedom will come soon enough.

Still new to Arizona, my college career path suddenly took a hard turn in a different direction. That's when I discovered massage therapy as a viable career option. It wasn't hard to consider massage, as I was on my fourth or fifth major and still not wanting to do anything I was studying. I would be moving from a communications major to a new school that offered massage therapy. You can say it was a 180° turn. When the idea of massage therapy became a probable and tangible goal, it was as if I saw a light in a murky tunnel. A friend took me to a local massage school one night for an orientation on the school. It was then I knew that's what I wanted to do. Everything about it resonated with me. They talked about healing with your touch and helping people out of pain.

Massage therapy training was what I soon embarked upon. My hands were always put to work on my mom's shoulders, who said I had my Grandpa's gift. He was a massage therapist, too. A phone call across our great nation was next on my agenda. I called my parents and told them I wanted to drop out of ASU and go to massage school to become a licensed massage therapist. It took some convincing on my part to have their blessing. It's a most credible profession. They had higher aspirations for me and my career. They didn't know yet how the massage therapy profession had become more science-based and therapeutic.

At the massage school I attended, we studied anatomy, physiology and more to understand how the body works. Soon after our conversation, they not only relented, but lovingly paid for my schooling. My parents truly wanted the best for me and supported this new cause, even though they didn't agree with my choice at the time. Their support is remembered with a grateful heart. I attended two massage schools during my career. They were both credible and most helpful in my attaining my goals. The first school I went to taught many informative modalities that helped me become a credible and well-equipped massage therapist. It was in this school I realized I had a strong desire for helping people out of discomfort and pain. The therapeutic approach resonated with me.

A NEW DECEPTION IS INTRODUCED – REIKI

The school also offered classes like Reiki. At the time, I had no idea what I was getting myself into. My journey during this time was to discover what would equip me to be the best massage therapist. My motives were good—I wanted to help people out of pain. It was soon revealed, Reiki is supposedly a universal life-force energy that heals a person's body and emotions. All I knew is I wanted to help people get better, and this seemed like the next best step to accomplish this. The way it was described intrigued me. The thought of laying my hands on someone and seeing them healed excited me to no end.

There are three degrees to Reiki. I went as far as second-degree certification. During the second-degree certification, we were taught secret hand movements and symbols that give power to the healing energy. This universal energy is referred to as "thought forms"– something that allowed us to have psychic impressions. Back then, I had no idea I was inviting demons to myself, which came disguised as symbols and energy. At this time, I had no idea during certification this wasn't God working. Again, the enemy of our soul comes as an angel of light. My heart was to help. This form of deception was introduced to me as Reiki.

During this class, I had an out-of-body experience. This was not new to me. Before I knew the Lord, I was taken out of my body on a few occasions. It was during Reiki activation that I was taken out of my body down a very long hallway with two very tall beings, one on the left of me and one on the right. In this experience, they looked pretty, not scary like in times past. The room and hallway we were in was all white and well lit. As we walked down a long hallway, they told me I would be healing people. I was so excited and felt very special, but as I was to learn later, this was not what it appeared to be. Deception can be so subtle and seductive.

When we lay hands on someone and expect healing to happen, I know now, it's not done in my strength and power. Only through the name of Jesus, does healing happen. I learned later, these beings that appeared kind and gentle were a deception. There was no mention of God or Jesus in the experience. The focus was completely on me. It was all about me and what I would be doing. The tall beings were appealing to me, and what I would be doing in my own strength, my power. Unknowingly, I was inviting the enemy into my soul through being inducted into Reiki.

TRUTH REVEALED YEARS LATER

God is so good, though; years later, I learned when I pray in the name of Jesus while laying hands on the sick, they shall recover, and they do when I pray for them now, all in Jesus' name. It's all about Jesus and what He did for us. The enemy cannot create anything—he can only take what God has already done and attempt to deceive and distort. It was another testimony of how God used what the enemy meant for harm and continues to use it for his good. Since I have been walking with God, He always gets the glory for healing. The joy unexplainable occurs every time I pray for someone in Jesus' name, and I am beyond blessed to see Him carry out his word. Jesus heals. The enemy comes as an angel of light.[1] He was trying to seduce me and make healing about me and what I did or how it was the universe doing it.

THE ENEMY COMES AS AN ANGEL OF LIGHT

Why would anyone with any sense listen to a scary monster or a hideous creature? He deceived me by making me believe I was doing good. It was so subtle, and it took years for me to see the deception. My hands would get so warm and felt like they were on fire, and people appeared to be healed, or at least feel better when I would touch them. But the focus was always on me—me centering myself, me channeling the energy, me activating the Reiki symbols, and me healing the person with Reiki. It felt good to practice Reiki for a brief amount of time. The deception was attractive to me and I bought into it. The Bible clearly describes this practice: "For false messiahs and false prophets will rise up and perform great signs and wonders so as to deceive, if possible, even God's chosen ones."[2] It wouldn't be for several years that the word would become alive in me. The Bible doesn't talk about Reiki as a form of healing. It is my belief and understanding that Reiki healing is counterfeit and it is not from God.

It is a blessing beyond measure now to walk in the truth. In no way do I want any glory for God's healing. I am simply his kid who partners with God and believes what he says. He says, "by his wounds, we are healed."[3] When I speak the word of the Lord over people and believe it when I pray, he moves, he heals, and he delivers, all in Jesus' name. It's not all about me. There is a joy unspeakable when you partner with our living God to do His will.

THE GIFT OF REPENTANCE IS REVEALED

God has always loved me and pursued me when I was deceived. He never gave up on me. He did and does always want the best for me. The truth about Reiki wasn't revealed until several years later. God knew my heart was to help—he loves me, and I believe he wanted me to see him and receive his truth. The gift of repentance would arrive soon, and when the revelation of what I walked in came flooding in, that's when I repented for being involved in Reiki. I repented for practicing Reiki on myself and others. Simply put, to repent means to change your mind from sin. Romans 2:4 says, "Don't you see how wonderfully kind, tolerant, and patient God is with you? Does this mean nothing to you? Can't you see that his kindness is intended to turn you from your sin?" His goodness leads us to repentance.

ANOTHER WRONG ROAD

That wasn't the end of being led astray on my search for God, after my encounter with Jesus. My search for answers as to who God is led me to some amazing and wonderful Native Americans and their ways of worshipping the creator. The people I was blessed to know were kind and caring. Even though I called myself a Christian at this time, I still had no idea what it meant to be one. The truth was yet to be revealed. My heart was to know the truth, yet the road was about to point to more lies again.

Invitations to sweat lodges, pipe ceremonies, and something called Sundance had begun. The love shared with me from the Native American people I came to know was so real, and I felt at home with them. I have since had some Native American friends in my church in recent years past, and I told them I was a part of Sundance. I did share that it was many years ago and their eyes widened as far as they could go. They knew where I'd walked and how I was deceived. The story of how I was delivered from it too was important.

A supernatural event occurred one night during a sweat lodge (not one like the night I met Jesus). I clearly remember seeing a dark shadow of a small man running around the sweat lodge when the flap opened. It startled me—it was just like the scary creatures I saw as a kid. It was more deception. The lies of who God was grew during this time. Again, I had no idea I was still walking the wrong road. God was there, and he always showed up, no matter how dark the road got—especially when I didn't know I was in the dark.

For instance, I met Natives on the reservation who said they knew Jesus, and they would pray with me in Jesus' name. Still, I was immersed in a life that talked about Mother Earth, Father Sky, and more. We talked about treating others well. They were such wonderful people, and it all sounded so good. This was my answer, or so I thought, to help me heal the hurts in my soul and help others. It speaks of good, right? It all felt so right, yet it was still a deception.

THE TRUTH WAS BEING MADE KNOWN

My faith has nothing to do with feelings. During many of the Native American practices I was a part of, the focus wasn't on Jesus and what He did for us. The discovery of who Jesus was, was about to take off. Jesus died so we can have eternal life. The only way to the Father is through, Jesus. We are saved by grace, not by works. These truths had yet to be realized, even though the love I had for these wonderful people was real. They treated me like family, wanted the best for me, and I bless them.

While writing the tale of my journey, I asked the Lord, "why do you want me to share such personal parts of my testimony?" My sense is, he wanted my story told to help people know the truth. I was deceived, and if one person receives truth and is set free, it's all worth it. The word says the truth sets us free:

"By the blood of the Lamb and the word of our testimony."[4] It wasn't until I started to walk in the truth of who I was in Christ that I started to see healing in my soul. That pertains to our mind, will, and emotions. Yes, I was seeking to be healed from so many sources, mentioned above. Nothing ever seemed to have a lasting effect. If anything, I always felt empty and worse later. In a sense, I was filling a God-shaped hole in me with things not of God. I was about to discover that Jesus is my everything, he is my healer of my soul and body.

MY BOTTOM WITH SUBSTANCE ABUSE

My self-medicating during this time was increasing. Drinking alcohol was a huge part of my life from the age of thirteen to twenty-four, in an attempt to make all the nightmares and pain go away. During this time, an addiction to alcohol and sometimes illegal substances formed. Some may say I was born with the addiction, I don't know. This I know—I have been set free from all substances, including alcohol, and I have been sober now since March 15, 1998. Since the day I stopped it all, every desire was removed and the desire has not returned. I know this now as deliverance.

My bottom from alcohol occurred three years after my encounter with Jesus. Those three years were some of the hardest and most painful years of my life. The emotional turmoil I lived in was suffocating me. The same friend who told me about Jesus the night I encountered him had been dropping seeds about sobriety for the last three years. During one night of desperation, I heard him. He suggested strongly that I go to AA. The next day after I sobered up, I called a lady at his suggestion who had been sober for many years. She was my first sponsor, and she started to take me through the twelve steps of AA.

THE ROAD OF SOBRIETY LED ME TO GOD

I hadn't been to church yet and didn't know who Jesus was. In AA, I met some amazing people and made some of my first Christian friends. It was also in AA that I learned many principles of the Bible. It was in the very beginning of my sobriety when I went to my first church meeting. I was invited to a Four-Square Church. That church was the next step in the understanding of what it meant to be a Christian. It was there I confessed Jesus is Lord and asked him to forgive my sins and invited him into my heart. I will never forget it, when I was water baptized, I came up out of the water, and I literally felt new. I actually was given a certificate too, proving I was water baptized. Although I have no idea where it is now, take my word for it, it happened.

Wow, I was twenty-four, and I couldn't comprehend what had happened. I know now, the old man is now dead and I am a new creation in Christ. This was wonderful, but cleaning needed to be done. My soul needed healing, and my identity in Christ was just beginning to be formed. I believe God used AA for a long season in my life to help me, and I learned to help others without any expectation of anything in return. Early on in my sobriety, my sponsor changed. My second sponsor, the lady who took me through the twelve steps to completion, was a spirit filled Christian. I had no idea what that meant at that time. The sense that I needed a Christian sponsor was paramount. Putting my trust in her and the guidance from God was all new to me.

BAPTIZED IN THE SPIRIT

All I knew at this point was I had done the sinner's prayer before the pastor and people at church, I invited Jesus into my heart and was publicly baptized in water. This is where I turned from my old life of sin to a new life in Jesus Christ. The word started to mean something to me: "Put on your new nature, and be renewed as you learn to know your Creator and become like him."[5] Then my fifth step of the twelve steps was to be completed at my sponsor's house in a remote northern town in Arizona. After that step was completed, she said she wanted me to talk to her sponsor in Washington, DC.

The phone call was made, and I can't recall the full content of our conversation, but I do remember I enjoyed talking to her. She talked about being baptized in the Holy Spirit. This was brand new, and I was so very intrigued. I was hanging on her every word. After a few minutes, she started to pray for me, and then I was baptized in the Holy Spirit with evidence of speaking in tongues. As the scriptures say, "And everyone present was filled with the Holy Spirit and began speaking in other languages as the Holy Spirit gave them this ability."[6] It was wild—I remember feeling alive in the most real way for the first time in my life when I prayed in my personal prayer language. I felt that too when I met Jesus and was water baptized, but this was different.

She prophesied over me too, and said many things. All I remember her saying with joy filled laughter was, "Oh, my gosh you are going to be speaking in tongues a lot!" I had no idea what she was talking about at the time, but I sure do now. This was reminiscent of the days when I saw psychics, but this time I had the sense that Jesus was right there with us and she was speaking truth straight from God. She is a Holy Spirit filled Christian with the gift of prophecy. Today, I love singing, talking, and praying in my prayer language everywhere, and it is like a river in constant flow. Praying in tongues is now my personal prayer language. It is the perfect language between you and Father God: "For if you have the ability to speak in tongues, you will be talking only to God, since people won't be able to understand you. You will be speaking by the power of the Spirit, but it will all be mysterious."[7]

I TOOK THE BAIT

It wasn't until twelve years later that I would be moving in this gift of speaking and praying in tongues. Years later, the understanding of this gift came in like a flood, and that was when my relationship with the Lord began to grow at a supernaturally fast rate. The church I was going to was wonderful, but I did something that drove me out of the church. I took offense with people and circumstances. The bait was thrown, and I bit. The offense stopped me from going to church.

In retrospect, I can see how so many seeds were planted at that church. This is where I was introduced to my very first Bible and became aware I was on a journey with God. My understanding of God's word was new, and it left me confused and baffled. The Bible was overwhelming to me. I needed help with understanding the Word and what it meant to be a Christian. By now I had separated myself from any "walking" Christians, because of the offense I took. I had left the church and moved onto another sponsor in AA.

THE REVEALING

God never gave up on me. He is amazing and was in constant pursuit of me. A few years into the AA program, I met a sober pastor and asked him if we could start a Christian AA group. That's when he shared there is such a thing called a recovery Bible. My next stop was to the bookstore, and I quickly acquired one. The sober pastor then invited me to help with the Christian twelve-step recovery meeting once a week. It became my first Bible study in disguise out in the open. We always referenced the word of God in our recovery talks, because the twelve-step meeting was focused on the recovery Bible. It was amazing. For the first time in my life, I was now a part of something bigger than myself concerning God's word, and I felt at home. Helping others see the truth as they traveled their journey while I walked mine brought me so much joy. It was in AA our God was beginning to be revealed to me.

ENDNOTES

1. 2 Corinthians 11:14
2. Matthew 24:24
3. 1 Peter 2:24
4. Revelations 12:11
5. Colossians 3:10
6. Acts 2:44
7. 1 Corinthians 14:2

CHAPTER 4

WAKE UP CALL

SHOCK AND AWE HAD JUST ENTERED

Life was seemingly going great. I had several years of sobriety, eight to be exact, wonderful friends, and had built up a successful massage business helping some of the most wonderful people in Arizona. I had wonderful family and friends, and I was, for the most part, happy. Then another wake-up call arrived, one that was brand new. For the first time in my life, I stood completely still in my mind and body. Have you ever smiled after receiving Novocain on one side of your face at the dentist, only to have the injected area completely immobilized? This is what got my attention, only I wasn't at the dentist. The Picasso-esque appearance of half my face drooping looked back at me from my bathroom mirror one sunny morning upon awakening.

Half my face was numb and felt lifeless to the touch. It was quite noticeable, both physically and to the naked eye. I shuddered at my reflection in the mirror, standing there for what felt like an eternity. It was vanity, and the shock of the sudden change in my appearance that got my full attention. That morning, I had a massage client and thought it was more than ok to go to work.

I sought wise counsel from my client that morning as to what this could be. She is a wife of a very successful and prominent plastic surgeon. She called her husband, and they agreed I needed to go to the doctor, stat. It was her prompting that led me to go my general practitioner. She expressed urgency in the situation where denial and fear were attempting to invade. Before I could get down the street after driving away from her home, just as I promised her, I called my doctor and made an appointment. The appointment was set for within a few days of the call and that's when the tests began.

LIFE GOT REAL IN A WHOLE NEW WAY

My doctor gave me a series of muscle tests (neurological tests). I wondered why she was doing them, since I have never had neurological tests before at any doctor's visits. All I had was a drooping left side of my face. I mean, really, it would go back to normal, right? So I hoped. After the barrage of tests, she shared her concerns. With hesitation and compassion, the possibility of multiple sclerosis was mentioned. She emphasized that nothing she said was conclusive. I felt a quietness in my spirit that can only be described as God grabbing my hand. Terror and fear soon followed.

On the drive home, it was as if I was in a cloud, a cloud of unbelief. I knew in my gut that is what I was dealing with. The thirty-six hours before the doctor's appointment, my inner investigator had been activated, I found myself googling every disease it could possibly be. I don't suggest that at all. It was tormenting all on its own. When I came across multiple sclerosis on a website, I sat there pinned to my chair, because I knew it in my heart that's what I was dealing with. Multiple sclerosis symptoms were what I experienced for a while, but I always had a reason, an explanation as to what it was. I would rationalize and say, "I was an active kid, and the weakness in my legs is because I hurt myself in my younger years," etc.

I believe the Lord was already preparing me for this news. He would give me comfort that goes beyond any scope of human understanding. Then my doctor ordered an MRI, stat. She seemed concerned, and that's when I was catapulted into another new journey. Being in the tube was scary, yet I sensed the Lord's presence through the whole experience. The results came back fairly quickly—if I recall correctly, it was within a day or two. She called me on a Friday around 4pm, wanting me to come down to her office to hear the test results. I expressed that if there is bad news, I really would like to know over the phone, please. The thought of driving to the Biltmore in Phoenix, during Friday peak traffic to receive bad news, didn't sound appealing. I was coming from Scottsdale, and I had a lot of reasons as to why she must tell me over the phone. So I told her, but upon reflection, the actual truth was I did not want to wait one more minute for the results.

She might have known this and had compassion for me. She agreed to tell me over the phone. She then shared the reality of multiple lesions on my brain, twenty-two to be exact. I remember so clearly as if it was yesterday, a peace came over me. The Holy Spirit filled me with such a calm, and I said to her, "Doctor, it is going to be okay. God is in charge of this." I completely surprised myself, too. I thought, "Did I just say that?" I can only imagine what was going through her mind. I was so calm and consoling her about my almost-diagnosis. She was more concerned than I was. She was very caring and compassionate, and for that I am grateful. Perhaps she thought I was in shock or denial. I know now it was God's grace and His Holy Spirit showing up for me in a most traumatic moment. Here was a wonderful doctor sharing potentially devastating news with me, a young thirty-two-year-old woman. I had my whole life ahead of me, and she was delivering this life-changing news.

The peace of God was and is more powerful than paralyzing fear. That night, I had plans to meet a friend at a coffee house in Scottsdale, Arizona. I kept my plans—why would I change the plans, I thought to myself? My face had returned to its normal shape, my body felt great and in my mind, nothing had changed. I shared the news about having a diagnosis of multiple sclerosis with my friend, and she lovingly attempted to console and comfort me. In a most caring way, my response to her was less than soft. In response to her kindness, I said in a rather firm tone, "No, please don't pity me. I will win this fight." In retrospect, I realize fear was talking. Then I excused myself and went to the restroom to catch my breath.

THE FIGHT TOOK ON NEW MEANING

That's when I saw it—the "sickness" in my reflection. I knew I was discerning in the Spirit, but I had not seen it before in me. I said to myself with such fear, "How did I miss this, God?" How did I miss it? I was horrified. There is no other way I can describe it. Multiple sclerosis was staring back at me in my reflection. It was so dark, and it terrified me. For a moment, my reflection didn't look like me at all. It was a glimpse into what was trying to kill me. It was the enemy of my soul starring back at me. That was the night my life changed again, forever.

In a most profound way I was to learn later what I was really looking at. This put new meaning to the term an "aha moment." During what seemed like an eternity, while staring at my reflection in the coffee house restroom, a feeling of utter devastation attempted to overtake me. Just when I sensed I was going to pass out, that's when I felt a gentle and most powerful knowing in my spirit. It conveyed this message to me with a clarity, love, and power I had not known before that moment. "Rachel, you are going to be just fine. This isn't even about you." I had no idea what that meant at the time, yet those words still echo inside my spirit today. They were so gentle yet so powerful. I know that now as the Holy Spirit.

The peace and power it gave me remains with me even as I type this very word, years later. That very word the Lord whispered to me is being made manifest in many areas of my life, including with this book. The peace in knowing it was God talking to me gave me a sense of hope, a hope that would only grow and grow. That was the beginning of relying on God in a whole new, and most tangible way. It was in that moment I entered a deeper relationship with the Lord. I had the beginnings of an understanding what the enemy means for harm, God turns around for our good.

Before that day, God was the one who saved me, saved my soul, saved me from wanting to commit suicide and actually doing it. God saved me from addictions, from wanting to run and hide from my life, and so much more. It was then I realized I was striving and existing, not living. The diagnosis actually brought me to life. I know it sounds like an oxymoron, right? Please allow me to explain. I had a whole new perspective on what to fight for: my life. It meant something, maybe for the first time, and I knew I was worth something.

DIAGNOSIS WAS NEAR

The revelation that my life has meaning came flooding in. I had a purpose, and I had to fulfill that purpose. The idea of dying from this disease or being crippled was not even remotely an option. A few days later I went to the neurologists my GP sent me to, a female neurologist. That is where and when I had every "un-fun test" under the sun, such as; a full body MRI, Visual Evoked Potentials (VEP), a spinal tap (ouch!), and muscle tests.

The spinal tap is a test I conveniently blocked out of my memory because it was so very painful, with needle going directly into my spine. They emphasized that you need to stay perfectly still while the needle is going in, or you could be paralyzed. I know now it's rare for this to occur, but the fear was present. The thought of what could have happened, if I had moved while the needle was injected into my spine is something I conveniently blocked out of my memory bank. Before this diagnosis, the worst sickness and injury I had to date was bronchitis, or the occasional broken bones and stitches, so this was all new to me.

It was only a couple days later that I received the news (in person this time) that I passed all the tests. This was a test I would have been happy to fail. I had four out of five markers. In May 2007, I was officially diagnosed with multiple sclerosis and rather quickly, within weeks. I was told this isn't very common. They said this is simply a disease that takes more time and testing to diagnose.

THE SEARCH FOR HEALING WAS ON

It was then I became determined to beat this disease. So much of my determination was derived from my own strength back then. I had yet to know and discover that God is my strength. The sheer adrenaline that was fueling me was about to come crashing down. It was then I was given a miracle gift from a very special and amazing woman and client. This wonderful client covered all the medical bases for me. She had one of her assistants make appointments for me at Barrows Institute with the best doctors here in Phoenix, Arizona. She also had appointments made with the best naturopathic doctor in Arizona. Covering all the bases was my plan.

The woman who helped me was extremely influential, and I was given the royal treatment by both doctors during this shattering time in my life. I am forever grateful for her help. I was given appointments that normally take months to get. It took me days to sit in the naturopathic doctor's office, with his number one associate doctor. That part of the journey led me to travel down to Tucson, Arizona, only a ninety-minute jaunt from Scottsdale. I love to drive, so that was no big deal. Another adventure awaited me.

It was an amazing visit; the man who treated me was an MD and ND, and a Harvard graduate. He had such a kindness about him. He interviewed me for an hour. His understanding of multiple sclerosis was astonishing. He taught me so much. He told me he would consult with the head doctor, and they would personally write up my treatment plan. The plan arrived days later and was ten pages long. I was completely blown away by the information and attention to detail. Hope was birthed in that office. He spoke of life, but it was not the life I learned later as life with, Jesus.

CROSSROADS

I put my hope in man again—a mistake. Yes, God uses men to heal us, but my hope is in the Lord. Upon my return home, I had another appointment at the neurologist to discuss treatment. The naturopathic doctor's office gave me a list of questions to take back to my neurologist appointment in Phoenix. That was an interesting encounter, to say the least. The list of questions was designed to extract information that the lay person doesn't have knowledge of concerning the treatment they wanted to give me. I will never forget how the neurologists sat there with what I observed as frustration over the few questions I had about their treatment options.

They asked me with a visible change in their attitude, but with forced respect. They asked me, "Where did I get these questions?" I said the Naturopathic doctor's name, and they had no comment—only a blank stare that could have been interpreted as discontent. They certainly knew of him, because he is a world-renowned doctor. The questions helped me make the right choice for myself. They wanted to put me on Interferon, asap. Interferon has a lot of lovely side effects, which includes, flu-like symptoms such as fatigue, chills, fever, and muscle aches-for one to two days after an injection, with headaches, anxiety, and depression. Liver function can also be affected.

This is where my journey takes a strong turn to a different and another unknown direction. I sat there quietly as the doctors from Barrows Neurological shared their treatment program with me. All I could hear was chemotherapy and side effects of vomiting and sickness twice a month for the rest of my life. Tears were held back, but I wanted to fall on the floor and cry out for help. I sat there with what I perceived as composure. Only God could do that in and through me. Praying was all I could do. I screamed an internal scream, "GOD HELP ME!" That's when I felt His strength operating.

It was now time leave, so I gathered my keys and purse. Looking at the doctors, I was making it clear our meeting was over. Thanking them for explaining the treatment options, I told them I needed to take some time and think about all of this. The appointment was over at that point, and I left their office. The walk to the elevator seemed like an eternity, because we were on a top floor of the medical building that was several stories high. In actuality, it was only a few feet to the elevator. I walked to the elevator staring at the down button, trying not to fall apart and hit the floor in complete despair. I had never felt so frightened in all my life.

AN ANGEL ENCOUNTER?

Then a man came up to me and asked me if I was going down as I was about to hit the elevator button. I was stunned by his incredible beauty. Yes, he was absolutely gorgeous, but that's not what I mean—it was a beauty that spans anything physical. His eyes were like windows into heaven—they were the bluest of blue eyes I have ever seen, beaming with God's love. Softly, I said, "yes please." He pressed the button and gently ushered me into the elevator, while guiding me gently on my back. After he got me in the elevator, it stayed open what seemed like an eternity. He pressed the button I needed, and the door closed with his hand still in the elevator. He remained on the top floor as I descended down to the parking garage.

While staring at this man, I pondered, "God is this an angel?" The elevator didn't close on his hand. I felt such support and love from him, a complete stranger. It was a love I am aware of now that comes straight from God. This was only the beginning of my recognizing God, as he showed me who he is and how much he loves me. It was the beginning of having the revelation of what I needed. I needed his strength, not my own. I drove home from the doctor appointment heading east on the 202 freeway as in daze. That's when an automobile tire flew out of the sky. It was as if it appeared out of nowhere.

The tire hit the roof of my car and bounced off my windshield. I must have been going at least 70mph. When the tire impacted my auto, it sounded like I had impacted another vehicle. In disbelief, I looked in my rearview mirror and watched the tire disappear. I was still in what I recollect now as shock from the devastating news I had just received. I know there were no accidents that day on the stretch of highway (at least during the time I was there) I was traveling on during the time the tire flew into my car. When I got home, still stunned from by the news, I went to my room and lay in my bed.

Suddenly, my roommate was yelling for me to come outside. He said, "You didn't tell me you were in a car accident! Are you okay?" he asked. The roof of my car was dented only a little bit from the tire, and that's when the memory of what happened came flooding in. I told him that a tire hit my windshield on the 202. He looked at me with concern, and the reality that it was a miracle came crashing in. The tire hadn't gone through the windshield and come crashing into my car. I have very little memory of that day because the traumatic news had me completely stunned. I have searched out pictures of vehicles that have been hit by tires on the roadway. In a few of the pics I saw, the tires went through the windshields and the hood of the cars were severely dented. But we have a miracle-working God.

I do remember what I believe was Holy Spirit saying to me, do not take their medication. That resonated with every fiber of my being. Now, what do I do? I had no idea what that word meant, yet, "You're going to be just fine Rachel, this isn't even about you." More was being revealed and was making more and more sense, the longer I walked out my healing with the Lord. Yes, I said healing, because I received a miracle from God concerning the multiple sclerosis. Those details would come soon enough. I got home and remembered clearly that the naturopathic doctor had said, "his office would call a doctor located in Ridgeway, Colorado," and gave me a personal referral to go see her.

The Healing Adventure Takes a Turn Through the Mountains

She is the doctor who literally wrote the chapter on how to heal multiple sclerosis naturally in an integrative medicine textbook. She received the diagnosis of multiple sclerosis years ago and went from being in a wheelchair during her medical residency to walking just fine. She discovered a way to heal MS naturally, and that was my next step. It was so clear, I had to go to Colorado and see her. Her patient roster was full, but having the naturopath as my personal referral was how I acquired an appointment so quickly. I had the one of best naturopathic doctors in the known Western world and did everything she said to do, only to have it fail.

Several weeks had passed and I was off to Colorado. This is where the next part of my journey led me, to the doctor's office in Ridgeway, Colorado.

I packed my little SUV and hit the road by myself. The whole way up the mountain from every windy turn, with straight drops to the bottom of the mountain, felt as if it was a picture of my life. Another turn after another and then it happened—I reached the top of the mountain. In retrospect, going this journey by myself wasn't the wisest decision. I called my parents along the journey and told them I was by myself, and they were less than pleased. So much pride had to be washed away, still. It was late, and as there was almost zero visibility going up the mountain, some fear got in. The cloud coverage consumed the mountain, and it had to be the Lord who got me there. It was a beautiful victory. I found the inn shortly after I arrived in Ridgeway, Colorado. It was close to nine pm. After I checked in, it was already time for bed, and my appointment was first thing in the morning.

I remember waking to the most majestic land, with trees that appeared to have been there forever. Their stature spoke of strength and gentleness. The sheer beauty of it took my breath away. Sounds of birds and the rustling of leaves were a music orchestrated by God to help me dance in his presence. The first time since my diagnosis, I stood still for a moment and just breathed in the surroundings where my feet were planted. Breakfast is a faint memory, but I do remember feeling like I was walking in what I know now as God's amazing grace. The inn where I laid my head the night before was down the street from the doctor's office. I drove there in a cloud of peace. God had his hand on me the whole time.

When I arrived at her office, I checked in with the lady at the front desk. An excitement and hope filled me to overflow. Determination and expectancy were driving me. I knew I was going to be healed. That was my heart's desire. I felt this doctor was the key to my healing. I put my faith in a doctor, in her story, in her healing, in her medicine, not God, not yet. My name was called, and I was escorted to the doctor's office, where she invited me to sit in a very comfortable chair. We talked for what seemed like a very long time, although it was only an hour. She shared her story of how she was healed of multiple sclerosis. I sat there hanging on her every word. I said to myself, "I am going to do exactly what she does and have the same healing victory she has had." Nothing was going to stop me. I was wired that way, to never give up, never stop searching for the truth and to believe there is always a way.

MY NEW BATTLE PLAN

That's the way I always was. I give God and my most wonderful parents the credit for this. My parents were like this too, in their own way. They set a fine example of what perseverance and seeking out the right way looked like. The doctor outlined a daily regime for me that included a daily program consisting of one tablet of vitamins D 5000, two capsules of Neurochondria, one capsule of Pro-DHA (pharmaceutical grades), and a very low dose of estrogen from a private pharmacy in California. That's what she recommended, and I was all for it. I thought, "I can do this." She also outlined a specific diet for me, which was a no brainer, as I already ate a healthy diet. Basically, all I had to do was cut a few items out of my diet and I was good to go. The exercise she suggested was something I had already been doing. I was already athletic and worked out regularly. I felt like I was already ahead of this disease.

THE CHURCH INVITE I COULDN'T REFUSE

She then suggested something that I had never heard of before. She recommended an eastern treatment, and since she had cured herself of multiple sclerosis, I had to go and do this too. Everything she suggested I followed to the letter. This was obviously no different. It was an eastern healing spa that she suggested. Shortly after I got home from Colorado, I called the healing spa and made arrangements to go. The week of appointments at the eastern healing spa was made for a few months after my visit with her. My determination to beat this disease was ignited with a passion new to me. I was now determined to not let multiple sclerosis take me out.

A few weeks before I left for the healing spa, I was given an invitation I couldn't refuse from a new friend at the gym. Most of what I did up until that point was in my own strength. It exhausted me mentally, physically, emotionally, and spiritually. My workout was now a fight for my life, so I saw it as such. I would go to the gym and sprint around the indoor track like someone was chasing me and I was fighting for my life. Very shortly after that, this was brought to my attention by a new friend at the gym, who said, "I think you need to slow down." He suggested I was trying to run from what was happening. He made the comment that maybe I was trying to run from MS.

After some consideration, I had to agree with him. He was right. Running is all I knew up until this point and it was time to face this, except I wasn't alone—I had the Lord with me now. I didn't have that awareness yet, but it was to come, and soon. It had been at least seven years since I had been to church. This new friend at the gym invited me to a small group at his church. I must admit, if he wasn't attractive and single I may not have gone. God knew what it would take to get me back in his house. The invite to church was so appealing, I saw it like a bright light in a dark storm, and that part had nothing to do with the handsome man. I told him I would go, but after I got back from the healing spa in Colorado. That was only a couple weeks away.

THE DREAM THAT CHANGED EVERYTHING

The healing spa is where the take-off happened. The take-off was into the word God had given me months before: "Rachel, this isn't even about you, you're going to be just fine." This program at the spa was the next step, or so I believed. The preparation for the treatment at the healing spa was rigorous, and lots of fasting and prayer was advised. The prayer they talked about had no mention of Jesus. I added that on my own. The very demanding eating regime included, vegetables, soups, mung beans, herbs, etc. Details of the treatment are excluded because I know it now to be tied to witchcraft. This is my story, and God showed up at this healing spa. God can and does show up anywhere.

The first day at the spa after a treatment that lasted a couple hours, I went back to my room exhausted and laid down to sleep for a little while. A very vivid dream time during my nap happened. In the dream, I was being chased by a man in the house I was in. He was trying to kill me. I was running from room to room trying to survive this insane murderer. He finally caught up with me and pinned me to the couch. Pleading for my life. I screamed, "no you can't kill me, I have MS and I am fighting for my life!" He then pointed to a book that went from floor to ceiling, and on the top of the fifteen-foot book it said on top, "The Reasons Rachel Has MS." He looked at me with such hatred and asked me, "Do you know who I am? I stared at him with such bewilderment. It was then he screamed at me, "I AM FEAR."

I gasped in the dream and woke up suddenly, speaking out loud the address where I had encountered Jesus in my dream for the first time, where Jesus had saved my eternal soul eleven years prior. All I could do was repeat aloud while still in bed, "30 West Carter, 30 West Carter." It was then I called a friend whom I hoped would have insight for me. I asked him, "What does this dream mean?" He said. "I don't know what it means, but you will know what it means, by the end of the week." I had an entire week of treatments at the healing spa, two a day to be exact, including a few consulting appointments with the director/doctor of the clinic/spa. I followed diligently followed their requests, except one. It was suggested not to read anything at all. I read my Bible every day.

MY SECOND ENCOUNTER WITH JESUS

On the eve of the seventh and final day at the spa, the answer to my question "what did the dream mean?" was revealed. I cried out, where is my miracle God? The questions I had, had yet to be answered. My desires led to the misinterpretation of the dream. I thought it meant I would have a miracle by the end of the week. I believed I would be miraculously healed and leave Colorado MS free. I know now that was my hope. I laid on the floor of my room at the inn, praying and crying out to God. The water in my tub was being filled, and it was almost time for my bath. Part of the protocol was a bath every night, to be followed by an enema or as they called it, a basti. Not very exciting, I know, but I wanted to be healed so badly. Back then, I would have died my hair purple or pink if they said it was proven to heal.

I laid on the floor praying in the stillness of the night. It was so quiet, I could hear what I thought were bugs making sounds outside. Then, I heard a very loud knocking. I sat up shaken and looking around. Suddenly, I realized the knocking came from within me!? I was jolted up and said aloud, to an empty room, "Is that you, Lord?" It was then that thought, "Okay Rachel you have been in isolation for a week too long and it is time to go home." I then proceeded to go to the bathroom and enter my bath, broken and hurting inside my heart and soul, and so very desperate for a miracle. I was about to receive another miracle.

Just as I got comfortable in the bath tub, the encounter happened within seconds. I closed my eyes, and it was then almost immediately that an encounter happened with our Jesus. Another life-changing experience to date was about to happen. I lay in the bath, and with my eyes closed, immediately I saw an old wooden door about eighteen feet high and six feet in diameter. My hand was gripped on the handle. It was a door that appeared to be the only thing in my field of view, and it was surrounded by what seemed an eternal outer space. It was then I attempted to open the door, because I heard an invitation from Jesus.

Jesus said, "Let me in, come join me." His invitation was filled with an authoritative, comforting love that still stays with me. I knew it was Jesus inviting me, because I had met him once before when I was saved at twenty-one. You don't forget what it is like to be in the presence of our Lord and Savior, Jesus. I knew in my guts I had been in front of this very door before countless times. It was an awareness I had deep in my spirit, and every time I tried to open the door, with my hand still on the handle, I felt an immense pressure keeping it shut. The revelation that it was fear holding me there came crashing in. It was then while still in the bathtub with my hand on the handle, in that moment, I yelled, "No, fear, you cannot keep me trapped in here any longer."

Then it happened—it finally happened—the door flung open. I stood there looking out into space. It was so mighty and vast, and Jesus was there right there in front of me. I couldn't see his face yet, but I knew He was right there. He invited me to go with him, to join him in his presence. I felt such paralyzing fear, but He and His love was so much greater. Jesus could hear my thoughts and responded to them. I thought, "if I step out and join you, will I completely disappear into space?" With every fearful thought I had, Jesus would simply repeat his loving invitation, "come join me." The invitation into His presence is like nothing I had known before this moment. The security, the love, and the absolute safety was something I had longed for all my life. It was as if those three words, "Come join me," were packed with volumes of meaning and filled with an eternal love.

IT ALL HAPPENED IN A MOMENT

I took a leap of faith as I pushed through a wall of fear into His presence. It was then I took my first step into what I thought was nothing, except it wasn't. It was fullness, the complete presence of God. After accepting His invitation, I found myself standing side by side with Jesus. I immediately started to dance around with the innocence and joy of a child. I could not remember ever having been so free. I understand Luke 18:17 now in an intimate way: "I tell you the truth, anyone who doesn't receive the Kingdom of God like a child will never enter it." Although an adult, I had become a child in His presence.

It was then I ran back into the room. I had just come out of the realization of where the room was, and it hit me like a tsunami. It was 30 West Carter. It was the room I'd met Jesus in eleven years prior, the very apartment I'd wanted to kill myself in—the apartment where Jesus had come to my rescue the night I had my gun on my bed with the intention to take my own life. The Lord interceded for me on that night, and that's when I met Jesus in my studio apartment. When I ran back into 30 West Carter, I stood there for a period of time. I don't know for how long, but a second more was too long to be in there. I witnessed the prison I had been living in for all those years, a prison of fear.

Then I ran back out to where Jesus was. He looked at me and said, "why do you want to be in there when you could be out here with me?" He then invited me to "close the door." Still being very childlike and filled with joy unspeakable, I said, "You are so right." I ran back to the room that was suspended in space, this time not entering. I was outside of the big door, so I grabbed the handle and slammed it shut. Running back to Jesus, I knew my life would never be the same. It was as if I had the thought, "I want to be near Jesus," and I was there. The running was a perception. The freedom in that moment was just the beginning of what was to come.

Now, I was where Jesus was and took his invitation to hold His hand. We then started walking hand in hand down, traveling down a cobblestone road with beautiful light all around us in what appeared to be infinite space, where we were filled with love and the peace that surpassed all understanding. I asked Jesus with an excited expectancy, "What's next?" He said to wait, that he would come for me and show me what's next. He told me as we were walking and he was looking at my hand in his, "it would be like this from now on." The love that filled these words stays with me, even as I type this. Walking hand in hand with Jesus just took on new meaning.

The sense I got was all I had to do was think about him and he would be there with me. I also had the sense this is what forever would be like, when I was walking with Jesus. The darkness wasn't scary anymore, because I knew he was everywhere. The fear of the dark was still so pervasive and oppressive, until Jesus showed up. Opening my eyes after the encounter with Jesus, I lay there in the bath knowing God in a way that was a new beginning. It changed me forever. I now had the revelation of what had kept me a prisoner for as long as I could remember, and it was fear. This was only the beginning of walking hand in hand with Jesus. Nothing seemed impossible after my encounter with the Lord. Hope was birthed in a most new a profound way due to my second encounter with Jesus. The mere thought of going to church filled me with a new excitement.

The unexplainable excitement and anticipation to get back home and go to church for the first time in a long time was new to me. I was brimming with anticipation. Just the thought of learning about God, diving into his word and being with other believers was a whole new definition of excitement. God was guiding my life now with my partnership with him. Before the night I encountered Jesus in the bath tub, I sought God in so many places externally. It was an inside job now. The word of God was right under my nose. Life was now jumping out at me through the word in the Bible. Hope breathed into me, and with that I believe, came a propulsion into my destiny. The church in Scottsdale my new friend told me about was next, and that's where I began attending a small group. I made friends with some very loving and wonderful people. Never before had I participated in any church atmosphere like this.

Most of the people there were right around my age. It was a singles small group/ministry, with the focus on learning the word, outreach, and having fun. Loving it, I jumped in with both feet. Then I started going to church on Sunday mornings and evenings there too. In a matter of a few short months, I was now a part of this wonderful church. Small group Bible studies were so engaging, and this is where I started to fall in love with Jesus and the Bible. I had accountability and was growing quickly with the Lord. God was doing a work in me.

HOLY SPIRIT SHOWING UP, NUDGING, CONVICTING ME

Godly conviction took place, too. It was time to get right with God in a lot of areas. I had been sober for over eight years and had worked the program of AA. Where I received and gave a lot of help. God used this vehicle for a length of time to teach me so much, but I always knew there was so much more I needed. I know now that I needed Jesus. The more I learned about God through His Word, the more I became convicted with how I was living. I thought I was living a good life, and I was a good girl. Still, living my life my way I made a lot of excuses for how I lived, and it was wrong. I am not condemning myself, just being real. One major area I needed to address was having a male roommate. He and I were sort of an item in years prior, too. It was time to say good-bye to him and start living right.

There were other changes that happened, too. Living right is not a punishment; I know it now as a beautiful gift from God. He puts things in order because he loves us, and it's for our protection. John 15:2 speaks of the fruit of the pruning: "He cuts off every branch of mine that doesn't produce fruit, and he prunes the branches that do bear fruit so they will produce even more." He allowed the painful process of remolding me and healing me. God definitely heals what He reveals.

MOVING INTO MY DESTINY

About a year into my new church, I entered a Women in Leadership Development Program. That was a powerful and growing time for me. I learned so much about what it means to be a woman of God. It was extremely fruitful, and I am grateful for every woman in the class and all the leadership. It was a year-long program and it was life changing. At the end of the program, you were asked to serve in some capacity in the church, in accordance with your giftedness. That's when I had an idea to start a twelve-step program to help Christian women. Approaching the counseling department at my church, I asked them if they would be on board with my co-leading a Christian twelve-step group for Christian women. I was so excited about the idea. Little did I know, what was next would again change my life forever.

ENDNOTES

1. Matthew 19:14
2. Romans 5:3-4

CHAPTER 5

MIRACLES ARE REAL

MY DADDY WENT HOME WITH JESUS

The church gave us a green light on the women's Christian twelve-step group, and that's when a storm escalated in my body. I had virtually no MS symptoms and was feeling great in my body. Weeks before the group started, my dad had died on January 6, 2010. He lost his fight with cancer. My daddy died a day before His 70th birthday. I had spent three weeks at his bedside where he was in hospice at my parent's home in New York. My dad fought quite an amazing fight. I had such a good daddy—he was a truly good man. The days before he died, he was given so much grace. I thank the Lord for the army of people praying for my dad. He did receive Jesus as His Lord and Savior before he went home, and the peace that fills me with this truth is indescribable.

Two days before he died, I was sitting on my parent's bed reading a powerful prayer concerning my dad's salvation, sent to me in an email from a friend in Arizona. As I was reading the prayer, he sat up, and with his voice raised and distorted he said, "Stop it." It wasn't my dad's voice. At this point in his illness, he wasn't talking. I knew the enemy was scared. I could have danced around the room. I got up and went over to my dad, gave him a kiss on his forehead, and went to bed. The confidence that his salvation was so close grew to a level I had not known before that moment. It was the next day I believe his eternal soul was saved.

LIKE A TSUNAMI

Hours after my dad died, the MS symptoms began to manifest in my body with a rapid vengeance. I know now why the symptoms got worse. I didn't know it then, but from what I learned later, I believe it was the spirit of death that got in me when my dad died. I don't know how this all happened, but I know how sick I got. One could say the trauma from my dad's death brought on the MS symptoms, but at this point, that notion seemed somewhat irrelevant. The peace I had after my dad died can only be described as God. I knew his immortal soul was saved, and I would see him again one day.

Literally, the day he died, the pain in my body manifested and was so horrible, I could barely stand it. The weakness in my arms and legs was increasing every hour at a frightening and rapid pace. The vertigo showed up overnight, too, and was worsening with every hour and every day. It felt like my organs weren't working correctly. That is the oddest sensation. It is almost indescribable. The pain in my body was almost unbearable. I was now holding onto walls and other immovable structures just to move around successfully.

I stayed an extra week in New York before heading home to Arizona. My dad's funeral was beautiful, and so many people loved him. I thank God for the many people my dad's life affected in such a wonderful way, mine most definitely included. I had the best dad ever. My childhood best friend met me at the mall so I would be properly attired for his funeral. That shopping trip goes down in the history books as one of our exciting adventures. There were many in years past. This one, I would be okay with deleting. The pain was so horrible in my body that my ability to walk was waning rapidly, and lifting my arms up over my head felt like an Olympic event. The vertigo most likely made it not safe for me to drive. I thank God for keeping me and others safe on the road that night. My friend was kind enough to meet me at the mall with an hour's notice, as she now had two little kids at home.

I NEED HELP

The week flew by and I was eager to get home to Arizona. I remember calling my friend Ryan back in Arizona and asking him to meet me at the gate upon my return to Phoenix. I didn't believe I would be able to walk of my own accord to baggage claim. All I could think, in a rather emotional and overly dramatic way, was, "I am not dying in New York. If it's my time, I am going to die in Arizona." I was beyond perplexed. Why was I having these horrible and morose thoughts? Fear was invading. This was before I learned about taking each thought captive. All I knew in my knower was, I had to make it home to Arizona.

Making it to baggage claim on my own and barely making it there upright, I could hardly walk on my own. I remember willing my legs to move as I walked through the airport. With my limited knowledge, I thought my tenacity and/or stubbornness was how I made it home from the airport in my own strength that day. It was actually the grace of God. It was His strength moving in and through me. He helped me move before I knew it was him helping me. Then it began—it was now a daily fight—a fight to walk normally, a fight to remember the simplest things, a fight to stay awake, a fight to not hit the floor and scream out in pain.

BEFORE THE MIRACLE

All the while, I knew I needed help quickly. Before I conceded and asked for help, a trip to the grocery store was like an Olympic event and not as a spectator. Mapping it out, I would only go to a grocery store around the block in fear of getting my car pulled over by a policeman. I was safe to drive, but walking without falling over was my challenge. A mission to find the grocery store shopping cart began, I would scout out the parking lot for a cart and park next to it. The cart is what held me up as I shopped. When I got back to the car, I felt as if I had run a 10K. Persevering seemed like my only option. What other solution could there be? Relying on my own strength is all I had known up until then. I had yet to learn to ask for help.

Upon arriving home shortly after my dad died, a few weeks later we started the twelve-step group for Christian women at my church. This is where I simultaneously started a class called "Pathways to Global Understanding." It is a class that educates and equips people to become missionaries. I wasn't going to let MS stop me from living the life God intended me to live. At this point in my life, I thought I was called to the mission field. Learning all I could learn and prepare was next on the agenda. My mission trip to Romania several months prior is what made the dream of traveling the world to help people a reality.

All the while, I was getting sicker every day. I had many dreams and I wasn't going to let MS stop me from fulfilling them. What was most challenging was the pain in my body, losing cognitive function, vertigo, and the ability to walk, which was waning rapidly now. The simplest of details would escape my immediate memory. It was quite humbling. For example, I would ask, "where did I put my brush that I just laid down on the counter?" I was always told by family, professors, and others that I was highly intelligent. At least that's what all the tests reported that my parents had me take as a kid.

Multiple sclerosis has nothing to do with intelligence or lack thereof. MS is a corrosive disease that chews away with lesions on your myelin sheath, that is the protective coating to the nervous system. The sense that God had so much more for me only grew, while meantime my body was breaking down. That made no sense to me, but I believed it despite what I was facing. It was there at the missionary equipping class, "A Pathway to Global Understanding," I met a nice lady who told me about how she was delivered and healed of epilepsy. She told me about a ministry here in Phoenix that could help me. It was obvious to the naked eye now, I was dealing with a severe physical battle. She believed that I would be healed.

After she told me a little bit about what to expect from the ministry when I went, I thought, "She's out of her mind." She told me that Christians can have demons, and that sickness can be caused by demons. She said demons can be in your soul, not your spirit when you are saved. She told me I needed deliverance from these demons and I then would then be healed from multiple sclerosis. Basically, I had very little to no understanding of what she was talking about. I knew about demons, because they had tormented most of my life, in my dreams, outside my window as a child, and at many of the places I went, until the night I met Jesus at twenty-one.

Her tales of this deliverance ministry now had my full attention. It seemed the sicker I got, the more desperate I became. After some gentle encouragement from her, I finally said yes, I would go. It was a whole week away until the prayer meeting. I was crawling out of my skin those very long seven days. I picked a verbal argument with her, even though she was my new friend. It was what I know now as manifesting. This was completely out of character for me. I praise God for her—she knew it wasn't me and had huge amounts of grace for me. It was the enemy attempting to divert me from being there, and she knew this. It had been six months since my dad died, and by this point, I wasn't able to work. I thank God for my mom and her generosity, who helped me financially during one the hardest times in my life. Without her help, I don't know where I would have been living.

THE DELIVERANCE VAN

Days before the Friday night of my miracle, God was shouting to me what I needed. God was on the move. It was like a megaphone showed up one afternoon, screaming, "you need deliverance." Right before I was delivered of multiple sclerosis, I was driving around old town Scottsdale. It was a mid-week summer day which meant not many people were on the road. In our hot season, Arizona is a less populated area. In retrospect, I most likely shouldn't have been driving. I thank God for keeping me and others on the roadway safe. My body was starting to shut down rapidly. This was the second time I saw a certain van.

The first time, a few weeks prior, it was on the roadway and drove past me rather quickly. This time, it was parked right in front of me, we were the only moving autos on the street at the time. The van was plastered in Bible scripture and it had had a phone number for the ministry, saying to "call if you need deliverance." I remember sitting there in my car and crying my eyes out because I knew that's what I needed. My guts were screaming, "this is what you need." Deliverance was so brand new to me, but I had the Holy Spirit living in me. He was talking. Interestingly, no one in the deliverance ministry I became acquainted with had heard of this deliverance van. This would be the last time I saw this van. My miracle was days away. Deliverance is something I had heard about a few times over the years. I was always interested to know more, but never investigated it, until now.

FROM DEATH TO LIFE IN MOMENTS

The Friday night arrived, and my new friend picked me up for the healing/deliverance ministry. I was unable to drive safely at this point. We walked into the ministry where I was helped into the building by her and her friend Melissa, who is now a dear friend of mine to this day. I needed help because my legs would give out with every attempted step. The vertigo was pervasive too; my world danced around me. Taking steps with the strength that was left was most challenging. She guided me to a chair up in front—she must have known that was the perfect place for me. Fear was filling me because of these new surroundings. Thoughts of crawling out of there and somehow making it home on my own invaded my mind. Basically, I was envisioning crawling down the freeway home.

Then it began. My recollection of the night includes a man sharing about what deliverance is and leading us in repentance prayers. Something must have clicked, although I couldn't tell you anything he had said that night. It was shortly after he led us in repentance that he started to command demons to come out of us. It was a dark room, and people were yelling, spitting into buckets, crying and using Kleenex to wipe their faces. Fear had me pinned to the chair, or was it Holy Spirit? I sat there wanting to flee with every part of me. The man who was leading the service took us through repentance prayers. I believe I started to repent out loud, and that's when it happened.

HOLY SPIRIT IS ALL OVER ME

I screamed very loudly, "Oh dear God I have twenty-two lesions on my brain. God, no, you can't take me the same year my dad died. That's too much for my mom." That's when a beautiful woman who worked for the ministry walked over to me and said, "Don't move, Holy Spirit is all over you." She then whispered in my ear, "The Lord healed me of MS in '08." That's when I almost fell out of my chair. Awe and wonder consumed me in that moment. Never had I heard such a thing. God was able to heal? Even incurable diseases? This was brand new to me.

Sitting there in my chair, I was weeping with uncontrollable tears as I was being delivered and healed from Multiple Sclerosis symptoms. Everything and everyone around me seemed to disappear. Peace was about to fill me like never before. Sitting there in the chair, I felt like my body was so light and I could almost float! Some moments later (the amount of time I was sitting there eludes me), I got up from the chair brand new. I walked on my own strength, which had returned 100%, and I was notably healed. I was beyond stunned, yes, but I was also healed. God had healed me. This made no sense to my carnal, conscious mind. I was now a walking miracle.

WALKED OUT IN VICTORY

Literally walking out of the service that night without any help was a victory that will always remain with me. Clarity of mind I had not known before that moment was now present. That night, people started talking about me being a walking miracle. I had heard of miracles before vaguely, but to experience it first hand, was an experience that made God even more real than I had known him to be until that moment. The friend who took me to the healing service and my new friend Melissa and I ventured to Pita Jungle that night to celebrate this most amazing miracle God gave me. Pita Jungle is a food establishment I use to frequent, the perfect and only place to celebrate.

It had been a while since I had been able to enjoy a meal out with friends. I sat there in disbelief that this healing had even happened. I apparently was questioning and speaking aloud, "Did that really just happen?" right after I'd just received my miracle. It was a harmless word I was uttering, or so I thought. I thank the Lord for these godly women who spoke truth to me. They said, "the enemy is sneaky and he was trying to steal my healing with doubt and unbelief, he is the father of lies. You must reject the lies." Wow, I did just that. That was the night I had the revelation of the power in our words. Fast and furious best describes my next part of the journey to know more of the truth. A whole new world was just opened up to me.

GOD'S HEALING POWER

More of what this ministry offered was what I needed. Two days later, I went back to another service there on Sunday night. This was where the mild symptoms I had were prayed away. That weekend marked a turning point in my life that has catapulted me into my destiny with God. Celebration after celebration was happening. Friends and family were rejoicing with me. Personal witnesses to my sickness and then my sudden miracle healing left them aghast. We have wonderful hiking here in Arizona; a milestone marker occurred one month after my healing.

A wonderful friend of mine and I went hiking on what we found later to be a 112° summer day. Multiple sclerosis and heat don't get along. This hike spoke of the evidence of my healing. The strength that flowed in my body with every step brought me to tears of joy and gratitude. That day brings a smile to my face every time I share the story. It was evidence of God's healing power. It had been a few years since I had been able to move with such ease and strength. I hadn't realized how much I had to fight with every step, even when I told people I had no symptoms. That's when I realized I wasn't being completely honest. Denial showed its ugly face, but I was still fighting MS with everything I had. It wasn't until God showed up and healed me that I realized he is the one fighting for me. It's his strength in and through me that makes it all happen.

Every day was now a celebration. Just to walk up and down my stairs at home and not wonder if I was going to collapse took me to my knees on my carpets at home, where I praised and thanked, God. I remember a moment, I was walking up the stairs of my home with full strength in my legs, vertigo was gone, the pain was gone, mental clarity and cognitive processes were fully restored and full use of my arms and hands were back. That moment seems so surreal today, but it was so very real, and it makes every step, thought, client on my massage table, workout and so much more that much more rewarding. I shared of God's healing power and how He gave me a miracle with everyone that would hold still, if they had ears, they most likely heard me give God all the glory for what He did for me.

MY LIFE POST-MIRACLE

This next leg of the journey began. The unveiling of lies I believed and the flooding in of the truth was about to happen. This part of the journey was more painful than any physical discomfort caused by MS, and I wouldn't change one moment of it. It was and is forming me, shaping me and molding me into God's design. The next leg of the journey consisted of my going to this ministry. There I was prayed for and experienced a lot of deliverance.

This was the beginning of my learning everything I could get my hands on about what the word of God says concerning deliverance and healing. So much truth and deliverance were shared and experienced there, concerning what I had gone through as a young girl and in my younger adult years. The things that were operating in me, that weren't me, I was delivered from too. That included deliverance from, rejection, rebellion, self-hatred, ungodly relationships, all the witchcraft I was involved in, and everything ungodly I involved myself in and more. This went on consistently for several months. Now, I practice self-deliverance on myself when needed. Basically, I live a life close to Jesus now. I repent when I need to, and if anything came on or around me that was not of God, I command it to go in Jesus' name. The deliverance part of the journey could be three books.

Knowing it's his Holy Spirit running through me, not the counterfeit spirit operating anymore, brought a peace and a closeness to God like never before. My identity in Christ was truly being formed. At this ministry, I discovered that the scary creatures from my childhood were actually demons. It made sense. The revelation of this brought so much healing. It was here I saw the great deception I had lived in and was being set free from. Peace now filled me in the quiet of the night. My deliverance journey covered my short lifetime of events, sins I was previously engaged in, my family line, etc.

I learned there too that the demons only have the power I gave them, by believing their lies and sinning. This is where I learned about the gift of repentance, too: "Now repent of your sins and turn to God, so that your sins may be wiped away."[1] Basically, to repent means to change your mind. When I started to walk a lifestyle of repentance and seeking God in all I do, my life began, and my identity in Christ started to make sense. Turning away from sin and repenting took access away from the enemy to my life and my soul, which consists of my mind, will, and emotions.

The Lord reminded me of the time when I first met him and he sucked the scary creature away from me, which turned into a bug the size of a fly. Demons are really not big and scary. The truth was setting me free. I was then asked to start working there by praying with the people only weeks after I was healed. Serving there was a short and blessed season. This ministry was a monumental gift that catapulted me into the next phase of my life with the Lord. My search for God's presence didn't stop there. Changing churches was the next thing I was led to do after I had my miracle. The ladies from the Christian twelve-step group where I used to go to church were witnesses to my healing, and so was my co-facilitator. It was time for me to find another church where they walked in the full gospel, so I said goodbye with love in my heart and I blessed everyone there.

GOD CALLED ME OUT

That's when I discovered CFTN in Central Phoenix, Arizona. There was a wonderful couple at the healing ministry who invited me to CFTN for the first time. The very first time I attended CFTN, I knew I was home. CFTN is a very special place that I am blessed to be a member of to this very day. The senior pastor actually called out someone for healing from MS my first time there. I didn't know what to do, since I had never been to a church like this before. The nice lady who invited me to the church walked me down front for the pastor to pray for me. There were so many people there that I was intimidated and so grateful for her loving support. All I remember was him saying something about miracles and giving me a powerful prophetic word. I fell down onto the ground, which I know now as the power of God taking you down. This was just the beginning of many more wonderful encounters with the Lord.

CHURCH WAS ALIVE

At CFTN, I delved into many classes that help you know who you are in Christ, your gifts, your destiny, and more. With both feet, I jumped into serving at CFTN. Helping out with the homeless teenage ministry was next. That was one of the truest blessings I have ever been a part of. To reach one of the young adults spoke volumes I cannot fully comprehend to date. Also, there was a church called Heaven's Place that was instrumental in my walk with the Lord. That is where I met a most amazing pastor who loved on me, poured into me and took me to her home country of South Africa half-way around the world. That was a trip of a lifetime. I am forever grateful to her for the opportunity to travel around the world with her and another new friend. I was so hungry for more of the Lord and what his truth was all about.

My spiritual eyes were open in a whole new way. I had been to Romania a few years before on a short mission trip, but never had I seen God move like he did when I went to South Africa. The fire in me for more of Him was just now moving. The gifts of God were being revealed. A few months later, I attended the School of Kingdom Purpose at CFTN. It was a nine-month long program/school that catapulted me to my next phase with the Lord. It was there I was taken through so much heart healing and revelation as to who I was in Christ. This was a time of walking in more of His truth. The teachings were always from God's Word, His people, and His Spirit leading. It was a truly powerful and a healing time in my journey.

IDENTITY TAKING FORM

Before I attended this school, I had no idea God was a God of grace and love. I had thought he was disappointed with me, because of some of the poor choices I made along my road of life. I had no idea, and because of this lie I believed I lived in condemnation. It was during this time that I was set free from these lies, and scripture started to become alive: "So now there is no condemnation for those who belong to Christ Jesus."[2] I heard this word for many years, but it was just now taking root in my heart. I then started to fall in love with Jesus in ways I never knew possible. I had heard that it's all about a relationship with Jesus, not a religious thing. Being a child of God and knowing this truth has only deepened my relationship with him.

It was another beginning of knowing Jesus and wanting the fullness of who he is. The Lord invited me into a relationship with him when I confessed him as Lord and was filled with the Holy Spirit. That relationship grows with every moment I am blessed to have with him. Partnering with God is the truest and most amazing adventure to date.

ENDNOTES

1. Acts 3:9 19
2. Romans 8:1

CHAPTER 6

WALKING IT OUT WITH JESUS

FEAR CAME CRASHING IN

Nine months after my miracle, the multiple sclerosis symptoms came back with a vengeance. They were worse than ever as evidenced by the increase of lesions seen on my MRI. I called Mary, the lady who prayed for me the night I was healed and delivered of MS. I was filled with utter desperation, confusion, and fear. Fearful thoughts came crashing in. How could this happen? How could I lose my healing? What's happening? I went from knocking on death's door to complete healing in a matter of seconds. I know it was true. I lived it, and I walked it.

There were many witnesses to that reality, too. Jesus had healed me. I wanted Mary to tell me how to handle this spiritually and practically. That's when the last thing I thought she would suggest happened. She shared with me about her neurologist she used to go to. A very deep breath is what happened next. Yet, this time was different. I had been touched by God in an undeniable way. The fight to not accept the lie that I was sick began. I didn't understand the word like I do now, but God was still with me. I was desperate and needed help again.

She and a couple others who had become wise and loving counsel in my life thought it would be wise for me to go to the neurologist. These people were Holy Spirt filled believers and walked so closely with God. Feeling defeated so much, fear was invading. my world came crashing in on me again. I listened to them, made an appointment at the neurologist's office, and miraculously they had an opening that day, which is incredibly rare for this doctor's office. It typically takes weeks to get an appointment with him. As it turns out, the doctor I had the appointment with was the father of the doctor who diagnosed me a few years prior. A very small world indeed—I was already in the computer system and that had opened a door for me.

Larry, a man who became a spiritual dad to me, took me to the doctor appointment. Some assistance was needed, and he helped me walk into the doctor's office. Walking was challenging. The wild thing is, I was feeling the symptoms worse than ever. Yet, I knew my issue was spiritual, and God was the only doctor who could give me a permanent solution. I listened to my new neurologist sharing with me about his suggested treatment to keep symptoms at bay. There is not a medical cure for MS yet. I agreed to another MRI, and the test showed quite an increase in lesions. I still didn't want to take their medication. I shared with the doctor, "I got this, thanks for your medical opinion." Research on the medication they wanted me on left me in turmoil.

LEARNING HOW TO REJECT THE LIE

In a matter of days, symptoms had rapidly increased, and I ended up in the ER. The ability to walk was rapidly leaving me, and this time it this happened within hours. This was new to me, with more rapid and severe symptoms. While at the hospital, I smiled at the attending doctors with a grace and peace only God could give. The people in my life now were all praying for me. They were visiting me in the hospital, commanding MS (the enemy) to leave me, and commanding healing to my body, in Jesus name.

The fight was on again and I was going to win again—nothing else was acceptable.

This was all before I learned how God has already won the battle for us. "The Lord himself will fight for you. Just stay calm."[1] The reality is Jesus died for us. He took all our sickness, and I was already healed 2000-plus years ago. This truth takes on deeper revelation with every day. This time, I knew who was doing the fighting.

When physical therapy came in to do their assessment the next day, they had a notable look of astonishment. They could not believe I was the same patient who had been admitted the night before. My progress was simply amazing. Strength had returned overnight. I remember holding back a flood of tears and thanking Jesus. Great news—I was discharged that day. It was all becoming real, in a way I could only have ascertained through my experience. I only had a twenty-four hour stay this time. God gave me another fresh wind of hope. My next step was to take their medication as prescribed. It was a five-day dose of intravenous steroids. I didn't want to put the chemicals in my body, but I felt it was the wisest thing to do at the time. The steroids are powerful and affected my body greatly.

SAYING YES TO THEIR MEDICINE

A few days later, I met with my neurologist again, and this is where he recommended preventative MS treatment. It is an infusion you receive costing roughly $5,000 a month. That's why good health insurance was essential. For that I am grateful. I did some more crying, and quiet and not-so-quiet wailing, as I conceded to take their medication. I was told by some very wise counsel and Spirt-filled believers, "God can heal you while you are taking the medication, and you will know when you don't need it anymore." Now, please understand I had no idea what that statement meant at the time. It did bring me hope. I shelved it for months, and I asked Daddy God, "what does that mean?"

During this time, I was going to the infusion center for the treatments once a month. My latest MRI states I have no active lesions, praise God. When lesions are active on the myelin sheath, that's when symptoms can occur. It was then I sensed Holy Spirit telling me I would be done with the infusions soon. Every month, I would go to the infusion center out of obedience, all the while asking God in prayer, is it now? Can I stop taking the infusions now? After a few months of my impatience, I settled into trust. Peace returned and as a result, my faith grew.

THE RELEASE HAD COME

Then the time came when I believed it was time to stop taking the medication. I sat there in the infusion center about to receive my monthly dose. The nurse who normally infuses me wasn't available, so I was going to leave. My experience with a couple of the nurses who worked there at the time left me in a lot of pain. They would miss my vein, and that caused excruciating pain—not an experience I would choose to have, especially if there are other choices available there. Calmly, I was sitting there deciding what to do. Do I wait for the other nurse to become available? Make another appointment or let the nurse available infuse me?

That's when "it" happened. The quietness and stillness of the Holy Spirit came over me in a most profound way. I sensed that beautiful nudging in my spirit again. It conveyed that I could go, and I no longer needed the infusions. My first response internally was filled with astonishment, "Really? Is that you, God?" And I sensed Holy Spirit conveying that I was done here. I believed I was done with the infusions. In faith, I got up from my chair slowly, and with a calm confidence I told the two nurses, "I am leaving, I am done with the infusions." To the natural eye, this was out of the ordinary. They were visibly concerned by my response to leave.

Walking outside, the sun was beaming down on me. I literally danced my way to my vehicle, crying with tears of joy shedding down my face. I left the doctor's office with more faith than ever before, seeing and watching God's amazing power being made manifest in my life. Now, a large part of my life had become about praying with people and sharing how God heals and delivers. Witnessing other's miracles too was becoming my new normal. When I pray for people, God shows up and healing happens. I can now remember what happened emotionally and physically without remembrance of the pain too.

SUCH FREEDOM IN WALKING WITH HIM

Such freedom, such hope remains. Please hear me, I am not a doctor, and I will never tell anyone to stop their medications. That is between the person, God, and their doctor. I believed at the time my faith had to get to a certain level before Daddy God would release me from the medication. This faith walk was so new to me. When I stopped focusing on the symptoms and started to focus on who I was in Christ, meditating on the word of God, believing what God says about me, about healing, living a lifestyle of repentance, commanding my body to be made whole, and telling the enemy to go, in Jesus name. My life and body were reflecting this.

FROM DEATH TO LIFE

Possible questions may be surfacing, such as "What is she talking about? What does she mean?" I will do my best to share what it means to me. I hear often how people are healed and set free, and their sickness returns. It has been my experience when my mind wasn't renewed, and I was believing that lying symptoms meant I was sick, the symptoms came back. Yes, I was healed sovereignly initially, but the symptoms came back and with a vengeance. Except this time, I was armed with the truth in His word. I believed was facing a spiritual issue and not so much a physical one. Yet, it manifested in the physical. The medicine can be used while God heals us. Yes, I do believe in taking excellent care of our bodies. I live and maintain mostly a healthy lifestyle, from diet to maintaining a physical workout regime. What I am saying is the root of the MS was spiritual, and I needed a spiritual solution. His Word was about to impart truth and life in the most experiential and powerful ways.

TRUTH REVEALED

Dr. Henry Wright's teaching and training on healing were next. Dr. Henry's teaching helped exponentially. One thing he talked about was the root causes of diseases. For example, self-hatred was a big cause of MS. He talked also about a crucial part of repentance. This was another ministry talking about repentance. More layers of the truth were being revealed. Self-hatred wasn't new to me, and I didn't know how to receive love from God or love myself yet. When my soul started to receive healing from these wounds that created the hurts, that's when life started to spring back. As layers were healed in my soul I began to walk out my healing in a more intimate way with God.

The truth was starting to fill me. Believing what God said about me, I am more than an overcomer. I am healed, I am loved by God, I am victorious, and he has a plan and a purpose for me and my life. My mind was becoming transformed as I started to believe what God's word says about me, not the lying negative tape player that played over and over most of my past life. Belief was a key, and the word was truly becoming alive in me. Believing the word and not a doctor's report, I chose to stand on the word, which says "By His stripes you are healed."[2] It doesn't stop there.

I chose to ask Holy Spirit to continue to heal my soul of wounds that happened over a lifetime. Another piece of this most wonderful pie is I choose to renew my mind with the word of God daily. For a long time, I had to listen to the word as I read it. I had so much distraction in my mind that it took this kind of pressing in for over a year to have quiet when I read the word. Now when I read the word, there is such peace, and I can absorb the word with my spirit. Discovering who I am in Christ is a loving journey. For so long, I listened to lies, but when this word started to come alive in me, everything became possible. His word is true and life, "because the Spirit who lives in you is greater than the spirit who lives in the world."[3] God is greater than anything the enemy throws at us. He said it right there—he is greater than the enemy. This truth was going from my head to my heart.

By declaring the truth in His word, I rebuked the lies I believed. A new way to start my day was to wake up and say, "Thank you, Jesus, for healing me." Especially on days when lying symptoms would show up. I say lying because that's just what they were. The enemy is crafty and uses things in the physical to attempt to take our eyes off Jesus.

REJECTING THE LIAR AND HIS LIES

Another round of this was about to start again. I was in perceived danger of believing I was sick again. I chose to stand on the word of God, by His stripes I was healed. Sometimes things take longer to manifest in the physical. It takes faith given to me by Daddy God to walk this out. I was now walking this word out: "Faith shows the reality of what we hope for; it is the evidence of things we cannot see."[4]

There were days when I would look at the lying symptoms and say what's going on, God? Why is this happening? I was there, I know you healed me. I barely walked into the healing/deliverance service with almost zero strength, dizzy and in so much pain, and walked out of there that night with full strength to my body and the pain completely gone. It was real, and there were most credible witnesses. I went from devastation to full restoration in a matter of moments. That began the journey to trust Him in a deeper way.

The healing journey continues. It is my heart to say that was the end of this fight, and I am living symptom-free. After about a year of doing so well with no symptoms, I ended up back in the hospital with MS symptoms, and more steroids were prescribed. It was confirmed by a prophetic word from my pastor "this was an attack of the enemy because I am walking in my destiny." He also said God uses doctors to heal; he didn't say not to go to the doctor. My pastor and a few others I am blessed to have counsel with is what took me back to the doctor. I fought with all I had and a lying feeling of being more defeated than ever invaded. Fear was present, yet I knew The Lord was with me. He has a plan and He was greater. Fear's eviction was served, yet I still needed to go back to the neurologist. He put me back on the infusions.

MORE MIRACLES HAPPEN

I didn't understand what was happening or why it was happening. Trusting in the Lord in a whole new way was about to transpire. It's been a few years now, and I am still taking the drug monthly and standing on his word that "the time will come when you don't need this anymore." My life has literally become an adventure or what I call a faith walk with The Lord. During the last several years, I have sought His healing with all that's within me. Beautiful healings happen when I pray for people, especially those dealing with neurological symptoms.

On one occasion, we saw an instant manifestation of God's healing. During the last attack that took me back to the neurologist, I prayed for a lady with neuropathy in her legs and feet. Little did she know I was dealing with the same symptoms as I prayed for her. It was only through God that I could stand at the alter that day and pray for her. After we finished praying, she stated that she could feel her legs and feet, and she received a miracle for our loving God. We celebrated in awe and the deepest gratitude of what our God had just done for her.

Driving home from church that night, I was laughing and crying, laughing, because of the joy of how God heals and crying because fear was still there. That night I took another stand. I made another choice. Weeping in prayer, I chose to look to Jesus and say, "I trust you Lord. I will walk this life out with you however you lead, my life is not my own, I gave you my life. I believe what your word says, Lord, I am already healed. I claim it in faith." Faith is believing before you see anything. I have now entered the most exciting adventure to date. Suddenly, after praying for this nice lady, it wasn't about me or my body working right. It was and is all about Jesus and wanting to fulfill the book written about me in heaven. His will not mine.

I BELIEVE WHAT HE SAYS ABOUT ME

God made me for this time, and he has a purpose for my life. It is my belief I am walking in that purpose today. Nothing could make me happier, living in submission to God and walking the road he wants me to walk. It's rarely about me —it's usually about helping someone in some way. This fire to do God's will comes from Him. He made me, and he fills me with vision. It is my prayer to be obedient and let my yes to him manifest His will. Not mine. May your Kingdom come soon. May your will be done on earth, as it is in heaven.[5]

Contending and believing for the full manifestation of my healing with no more lying symptoms is what I stand on and believe Him for. I'm putting my trust in Jesus and believing what He said is true. "Has he ever spoken and failed to act? Has he ever made a promise and not carried it through?"[6] His Word talks about how healing is ours. This left me with a confidence and strength that could only come from him. My faith muscles were getting bigger.

I was developing the strength of walking in faith, the strength of believing what he said is true, and the strength in partnering with him to walk this life out, with him leading the way. Trust was now a word with real life applicable experience. Trust was filled with a love so new and fulfilling. It was no longer a cute cliché. This word dances with new life every time I read it: "Trust in the Lord with all your heart; do not depend on your own understanding. Seek his will in all you do, and he will show you which path to take."[7] This walk has been everything, but boring. The anticipation for every new day is filled with hope like never before. Living the adventure I dreamed about is my current reality.

ENDNOTES

1. Exodus 14:14
2. 1Peter 2:24
3. 1 John 4:4
4. Hebrews 11:1
5. Matthew 6:1
6. Numbers 23:19
7. Proverbs 3:5-6

CHAPTER 7

FAITH WALK

HIS WORD COMES TO LIFE

What does it look like to walk out your healing? I asked myself this question in many ways more than a thousand times. I stood on the word, by his wounds we are healed. That scripture has come to life in more than one way. His word is truly living and active. Faith was now my way of life. During an attack on my health, I came home from church one Sunday afternoon exhausted. I cried out to God and said, "I am doing everything I can do, everything I have learned and I am not seeing your word manifest in my life the way I want it to yet." Fear and turmoil had invaded again. I laid on my couch with the sun beating down on my face. I did all I had learned up until this point, which was a lot, and I told fear to leave me in Jesus name. It came to mind that I needed to trust Jesus, believe his word and surrender all, again.

Sleep happened rather quickly, and I was suddenly in a place I have never been before. It looked like the heavens; the colors were so vibrant and alive. Then I saw myself from about 300 yards away with what looked like a group of spirits around my head. I knew immediately they weren't from the kingdom of God, because they looked like the creatures that had harassed me as a kid. I then charged at them speaking in tongues (my heavenly language). The whole time, I could interpret that I was speaking his word. "By his wounds you are healed," is what I was speaking.[1] As I approached my body and the spirits around my head while speaking in tongues, they started to scream and scattered immediately.

Waking up suddenly, I realized I had no symptoms in my body. Before I went to sleep, my legs and feet were mostly numb and weak. Upon awakening, I sprang up off the couch and total strength had returned to my body. Tears started to stream down my face. That was when I had the revelation about the word of God, again. It is truly living and active. All we have to do is believe and receive the truth. "Therefore I tell you, whatever you ask for in prayer, believe that you have received it, and it will be yours."[2] I believe when I charged the demons around my head speaking the Bible at them, that's when they scattered and I woke up symptom free.

NEW VISION

I wish I could say that battle was over, but it played out a few days longer. I sensed that the Lord was saying this fight was almost over. Lying symptoms came back around, not as strong, but there nonetheless. It was a few days later we had a prayer meeting at my church. This is where I was led to go and sit in one of the rooms by myself at the prayer meeting. Sitting there in a comfy chair, I started to pray in the spirit. Suddenly,

I started to live the dream I'd had a few days prior. I saw the enemy attacking me outside of my head, and I started to speak the word out loud in English now, "by His wounds we were healed."[3] That was a day of victory. I left the prayer meeting without any lying symptoms.

Faith muscles were exercised again. I call them lies because that's what they are. The truth is I am already healed, because of what Jesus has done. Anything else to the contrary is a lie. That includes all sickness. Seeing evidence of his word come to life again, lifted me up to a place where I could rest in the truth and not focus on what was happening in the natural. The supernatural is more "natural" and real anyway.

The word of God was becoming interactive. Another encounter with the Word was just around the corner. His Word is life; it is our hope. The living word was becoming a part of me.

BY HIS SPIRIT

Allow me to digress—I was on the way to a new client's home. I knew in my Spirit it was a divine connect. As it turned out I was correct. He is a pro athlete who happens to be a spirit-filled Christian. He allowed me to pray over him for many things, and God showed up big time, from prophetic words to the manifestation of healing after I prayed. Due to my respect for my clients, I don't share any personal details concerning him or anyone else. As I was driving to his home, my feet started to go numb. This was a thirty or so minute jaunt to his home, too. Instantly, I remembered the dream I'd had the night before.

It looked like a massive woman was on my massage table. She must have been nine feet tall and weighed at least 400lbs. When I tried to move the being off the table, I got close and looked into its eyes. I then realized it wasn't a woman, but a demon. That's when I became angry and tried with all my might to get it to move off my table, only to have it not move. It just looked at me, laughing sinisterly. I then started to yell loudly at it, as it wouldn't move in my strength. I was yelling, "It is not by force nor by strength, but by my Spirit, says the Lord of Heaven's Armies."[4]

I must have yelled this scripture at least a dozen times at the creature. Every time I spoke it, the creature got weaker, and then eventually it disappeared. Waking up, with no symptoms in my body, I knew it's God's power, it's his spirit, it's all him doing the healing and delivering. Well, now it's the waking time again. Driving to my new client's home, this fresh memory was flooding into me. This dream had happened only 24 hours prior. I started to speak that scripture over myself. It was so powerful—his presence flooded me and my auto. By the time, I got to my new client's home, I walked out of my car without any lying symptoms. All I could say to myself was, thank you, Jesus.

There was so much strength in my feet and legs, and I knew it wasn't my strength, but his, that got me there and sustained me. That revelation stays with me today, and it is a weapon of warfare I use for myself and others when I am blessed to pray for anyone God puts right in front of me in need. It's not me doing it in my strength, it's his strength getting done what needs to get done. When I am reminded God has all power, it brings me peace that surpasses all understanding. In that peace, I discover rest and His strength moving in me and my life. Basically, it's so simple. God does it all. He is the one who heals, delivers, and sets us free. We come into agreement with Him and his word, and it's really the best relationship I have ever encountered.

FAITH WAS RISING

During this time, I was on a second round of infusions for MS which meant going to the infusion center once a month. Faith would go to new levels every time I ventured there. What does that mean? Well, it wasn't easy, but quite doable, only because, He is always with me. On the day of the infusion, I would start my day praying, asking God, is this the day? Is this the day I can stop going? He has told me to date, to trust him and that he would give me the strength I needed.

Trust took on new meaning when I surrendered all to God. I would go to the infusions in faith that my healing would manifest completely. I still stand on the word, and still believe what Jesus has done. He has already healed me. Standing on the word of God and walking with him can be described as a contradiction, yet it's the most beautiful contradiction I live to date. What God says is reality. For we live by believing and not by seeing.[5] I see myself completely healed before it manifests in the natural. As far as I am concerned it is already done. This faith given to me by God fills me with such peace and hope.

My relationship with the Lord speaks of another tale now. One morning before I left my house for the infusion, I cried while blow drying my hair, asking Daddy when is this going to be over? He said to trust him, he will let me know. I then started to pray, covering the medicine in the blood of Jesus, nullifying anything negative and asked him to use me there. Every time I would go to the infusion center, I would pray and ask God to use me. He always did.

It happened a few times that I shared God's love with someone sitting next to me being infused. My heart sometimes would become overwhelmed with compassion for the people around me of all ages. I would cry out to God for their healing, for their salvation silently in prayer. The nurses here are straight from God, too. This office is truly one of the most blessed medical facilities I believe exists. Over the last few years, I have gotten to know some of the nurses there at the infusion center. The opportunity to pray for a couple of the nurses has arisen, too. Praise God, I have had the opportunity to pray for one of the nurse's family members who was dealing with a medical issue. The next month, a praise report was shared.

Facebook is a form of communication I frequent. One morning, I noticed my pastor had a very encouraging message he had just posted right before I entered the infusion center. I was led to share the post with a couple of the nurses. One of them came over to me and hugged me with tears in her eyes, saying she needed to read that. She proceeded to give me her phone number so I would send her the post. I know by the spirit of God these infusions are coming to an end one day. It is wonderful how God can use us amid what can be perceived as trying circumstances.

I have said to God, "Lord, if the whole reason I am going through these infusions is to pray for people there. It is worth it." I shocked myself, because I meant it, too. That revelation still speaks of the faith God gave me. This faith I talk about is a gift from God; I am not capable of having this kind of faith on my own. It's Holy Spirit helping me with every literal step I am blessed to take. In all honesty, if it were up to me, I would have rationalized my way to other decisions, dealing with much of what I have been through. Now, my walk with God is so simple. I stay to close to Jesus, hang out with him, read the word, pray and do what He says. I like this way a lot better.

MY NEW NORM

I have walked the faith walk now more times than these pages will allow. A few times I have awakened with weakness in my legs, not knowing if I was going to be able to function normally that day. The journey has progressed from me crying to God for help in a 911-reactive way, to me simply getting quiet before him, operating in what I already know now as truth. My faith walk is rooted more in the truth now during challenging moments. Calm and peace accompany me now in the battle, because the battle is not mine. The Lord fights for me, even though I still enact his word. What does my part look like? I speak healing scripture over myself, and I lay hands on myself, commanding all lying symptoms to go. I command healing to certain parts of my body, speaking prayers of healing over MS specifically, and believing the whole time, God did what he said he did.

He already healed me. On those days, I would ask God if he wanted me to go to clients' homes and work on them? Nine times out of ten he said, "Trust me, I am with you; I will give you all the strength you need." Then I would proceed to get ready for my day. Invariably that day was filled with divine appointments. Again, nine times out of ten, by the time I would arrive at a client's home with my massage table and accessories, all symptoms would be gone by the time I got out of my auto. With every step of carrying my massage table into my clients' home, my faith and physical strength grew by leaps and bounds. I was now living the scripture, faith without works is dead. "So you see, faith by itself isn't enough. Unless it produces good deeds, it is dead and useless."[6]

The days I had a battle were usually the days when people were healed, when prayer was offered and accepted. I had the best results, too, with the physical work I do—the days when salvations happened, or the days when the anointing was so strong, a word from the Lord was shared. Our living God was with me and helped me to do the job he set before me. What the enemy means for harm, He turns around for our good. My identity is in being a daughter of God, not someone fighting lying MS symptoms. That means, I believe what He says about me. He said I am more than a conqueror.

The relationship I have with Jesus only grows deeper with every step I take. This was also the beginning of understanding what it means to walk in the spirit and not the flesh, to walk in the truth, not the lies the world throws at us. Part of my faith journey so far has taken me around the world to a few destinations. God was with me at the local grocery store on all my overseas ministry trips, from Romania before my miracle healing, to my post-miracle healing, when He took me to both South Africa and England. All three of these trips were as different and as wonderful as you can imagine. Yet, the one thing that remained, is God is God everywhere. I get to take him everywhere I go. He lives in me. His healing manifests here in Phoenix and on the beach in Durban, South Africa.

<hr>

ENDNOTES

1. 1 Peter 2:24
2. Mark 11:24.
3. 1 Peter 2:24
4. Zechariah 4:6
5. 2 Corinthians 5:7
6. James 2:17-19

CHAPTER 8

THE JOURNEY HAS JUST BEGUN

LEAVING THE NEST

The anticipation of what God had for me only grew. It was as if my life was just getting started. By this time, the ministry I had worked in for a few years was nearing a transition. The ministry got word from the Lord, it was time for me to leave the proverbial nest. The ministry's leader had helped me and mentored me for a few seasons of my life. Wings drying as I flew from the nest, the next was right around the corner. This was a time of equipping. He had helped me considerably to walk in the truth. God had set it up, and he was the minister who prayed for us all the night I was healed of MS. I am eternally grateful for all he's poured into my life.

God uses his kids to help his other kids.

Literally, a couple months later after flying into new territory with the Lord, my healing journey led me to Joan Hunter's ministry. I went to her healing school and meeting she offered locally here in Phoenix. Life was going well, business was a success, and my body was doing very well, minus a couple of lying, annoying symptoms. Everything Joan taught on that week was exactly what I needed, but didn't know it yet. She prayed for me, for my healing, while she was here in Phoenix. How she prayed was exactly what I needed to know next. I knew this without any doubt. This led me to acquire her healing school teachings and get ordained through her ministry in Tomball, Texas. It all happened so quickly and powerfully, in a matter of a few months. God was in it. Confirmations from the Lord came flooding in.

EQUIPPING HAS GONE TO A NEW LEVEL

The support to go forward with the ordination from Holy Spirit, friends, and spiritual advisors was synonymous. I had been praying for people in my home town and now it was time to go to new places with the Lord. I was ordained through Joan Hunter Ministries and have had the opportunity and blessing to pray with Joan and her ministry team a few times. God moved mightily, and we saw many people experience healing. This was so exciting—I felt like I was walking in what God had called me to do. I know God is our healer, and my faith grows every day. My story alone speaks of this truth. Not only have I learned to trust God with my health and healing, I trust him with every part of my life. I truly believe I gave him my life to do with me as he wills.

I believe him. I am already healed, because of what Jesus has done. I choose to walk this faith walk out with Him. Joan's teachings were very directive on how to pray for so many diseases, particularly multiple sclerosis. She offers specific prayer protocols for many illnesses. A new battle plan was presented. At times, I lay hands on myself and walk through a certain prayer illustrated in her books. When I pray for myself, it is just as effective as any other Holy Spirit filled believer praying for me. A most beautiful truth in God's word is "you can lay hands on the sick and they shall recover."[1] That means I can lay hands on myself, and miracles can and do happen. The same spirit that lived in Jesus now lives in me. Basically, it's him in me who has already healed me. I believe and receive what he's already done for me.

There was a time when I woke up one Sunday morning and my legs were weak. Pushing through the moment, mostly ignoring the lying symptoms that morning, I spoke life and the word over myself and got ready for church. We have some of the best worship at my church that I have been blessed to engage in. That morning, I went right up to the alter and pressed into worshipping our God. While singing and praising our amazing God, I laid hands on my legs. I was saturated in his presence and was led to command all lying symptoms to go in Jesus' name, said a few directive prayers illustrated in Joan's book, and suddenly felt electricity through my whole body. Half-way through worship, every lying symptom had left. I cried and thanked Jesus. It has been moments like this that illustrate how He is the alpha and the omega. The best way I can describe that moment was a humble gratitude flooded with awe of how truly amazing and all powerful our God is.

In recent times, I have been beyond blessed to have some of God's most anointed men and women of God pray for me, men and women who have seen literally hundreds if not thousands healed and set free after they had prayed for them. I asked God, why is my healing not manifesting? I know it's God healing me and the anointed people praying are acting out his word. Don't get me wrong, during a season in my life my body use to respond almost immediately to their prayers and others. This does not negate their prayers. I still seek prayer from other believers. There is such power in prayer and the word of God. As James 5:16 states, "Confess your sins to each other and pray for each other so that you may be healed. The earnest prayer of a righteous person has great power and produces wonderful results." I have learned to walk in faith and believe Him at his word, not base my life on what I am feeling in my body. His word says I am healed by his stripes. It is done, it is finished.

After spending some time in prayer on my face. Holy Spirit led me to lay hands on myself. He moved, he showed up, and healing happened. The truth of how God heals was becoming magnified in the most intimate way. Perhaps this was a vehicle for more faith muscles to be built up. This I know with certainty—every battle brings me closer to him. I have pondered over the years, why does the enemy throw this stuff at me when I just grow closer with Jesus? I don't focus on the enemy anymore, because it's all eyes on Jesus. There is nothing that God can't use for his good.

NEW LIFE EVERYDAY

Every day is a new day. I mean that. I am walking it out daily, with him, one precious day at day time. I am in my early forties now, but my life has literally just begun. If you told me ten years ago my life would be the way it is now, I would have looked at you like you're an alien. The idea of living a life of faith, like I live now, was not a part of my reality back then. I wouldn't change a thing. Back then, I was trying to attain goals based on what Rachel wanted. In a sense, it was all about Rachel. Now, I partner with God and submit to him, which used to be foreign to me. It usually isn't about me, it's about helping someone right in front of me.

I literally can't see any other way to live. For most of my life, fear used to have such a dominant influence. Holy Spirit is my chief influencer now. I gave my life back to God many years ago. When I awake to a new day, I say, "Your will be done today, not mine." Each morning is new and filled with hope most days. My goodness, this was the antithesis of how I use to live. The fruit of being with God today spans my known reality. Patience, self-control, joy, and peace, just to name a few, are a part of me and my life now. In the years prior to walking with Jesus, those words had no meaning to me. The negative is what held true; fear, impulsiveness, sadness, and unrest were what poured out of me. I was truly lost before I knew Jesus. I had no hope. I thank him, because he came for the lost, and today I live from a place of hope. "For the Son of Man came to seek and save those who are lost."[2] Hope is renewed daily as I put my trust in him.

EVIDENCE OF BEING A NEW CREATION

Today is very different than in the years I didn't know Jesus, polar opposite, to be exact. I believe what he says about me in his word today, and that continually transforms me. I glean from who God is, and who He has made me to be. It is pure joy knowing and living the truth. It's not all about me. I am his creation, and he made me for a time such as this for a plan and a purpose. Those words have life now. Even as I typed them, I got excited, because I believe what He says is the truth. Every day is an adventure with God, he directs my steps. A trip to the grocery store can be a lot more than picking up coconut milk. I have had several encounters with God moving, doing my daily tasks. That might be a book all by itself one day.

A CARTON OF COCONUT MILK

One encounter happened one afternoon at my local grocer. A nice lady was standing in line behind me at the check-out line. I was there to quickly get my coconut milk and a few other items, or so I thought. She was holding several different products in her hands, very focused on not dropping anything. I invited her to put the items down on the conveyer belt and go before me. She paused and quietly said, "I can't, there are too many germs there." Immediately I paused and prayed quietly asking, "What is this Lord?" A conversation had now started between us. The gift of gab with complete strangers is something God gave me, since the time I could first make sounds, and he uses that in me all the time to the present day.

She then shared how her husband had been fighting blood cancer and his blood type had changed, due to a blood transplant. She also shared how his immune system was severely compromised and his body was having trouble accepting the new blood. She said she couldn't risk picking up any germs. I had no idea someone's blood type could change due to a blood transplant. Our conversation continued outside as we stood in front of the grocery store. That's when I offered to pray with her. I was led to share with her how I was recently ordained through Joan Hunter's ministry. She got visibly hopeful and shared how she had watched Joan Hunter on TV before. She then welcomed me to pray for her and her husband. Because they are married, they are joined together.

Jesus is the one who heals, but the association with Joan Hunter's ministry gave her some confidence that she was talking to someone she was more familiar with. I then prayed for her and her husband in the parking lot of the grocery store. They are young, in their early forties and have a family. We said our goodbyes, and I then left the store. A few days later, I received a text from her, asking me to come to the hospital and pray for her husband. Rarely do I ever give out my personal phone number to strangers, but in this instance, I was led to give her my contact info that day in the grocery store parking lot. A few days later, I received what I inferred as a "911 text" asking me to come and pray for her husband, please. She shared how her husband was in the ICU and not doing well. I made it a priority to go to the hospital and pray for him, believing in his miracle.

ANOTHER MIRACLE

Months prior in pre-ordination I had learned through Joan's teachings how to pray specifically for anyone who has received body parts that were foreign to them. Receiving someone else's blood to the point that it changes their blood type most definitely qualifies. This nice lady was sharing with me how her husband's personality had showed changes after the blood transplant. All my bells and whistles went off. It was like I was reading the segment in Joan's book pertaining to this directly.

I prayed according the book's protocol for what was ailing him specifically. It was so simple. It was Jesus—he moved, he did it. While I prayed, his monitors showed him calming down, but there weren't any other visible signs of improvement yet. Just the utterance of the name Jesus brought stillness and peace to all who were present. It was time for me to go, and I made my way to my auto. I heard from the nice lady the next day—her text related the best news ever. Her husband was suddenly out of ICU and was doing remarkably well. Reading her text brought me to tears. This is our God, I cried out loud, thank you, Jesus! Doctors were stating how remarkable this was. We know it was our God. The joy was unspeakable. With days like this, every day is truly the beginning.

That is the God we serve, a miracle-working God. You never know who needs his touch, and it is most likely the person right in front of you. It can be you he uses to love and pray for the person right in front of you. Sometimes it's the person you work with, your neighbor, your family member, or the kid working at Costco. One true thing is, people are everywhere. People need God, and I count it all joy to be His vessel. Sometimes it's a prayer, a smile, a word of kindness, a prophetic word, or to make someone laugh. The possibilities are endless. We have a miracle-working God who loves us so much and wants the absolute best for us.

REVELATION OF WHO HE IS

Did I have any lying MS symptoms while I encountered this nice lady at the grocery store? Honestly, I don't remember if I did or not. That is irrelevant. The focus wasn't on me. As a matter of fact, today I don't worry or focus on that anymore. Fear was given the eviction notice. I choose to stand on my faith, with all eyes on Jesus. In that moment, it was all about what God wanted to do for her and her husband. It's in times like this, there is evidence I have submitted my life to Him. I have learned not to focus on lying symptoms, too. The enemy would love it if I did. The more I focus on Jesus, the word of God, and the truth, the revelation of his love takes on new meaning.

It makes no sense to the natural mind. That is a good thing—a very good thing. A lifetime ago, I was programmed to focus on the problem and find a solution my way. I found out along the journey, the solution is Jesus. I relate it to walking out the word in Spirit and in truth with him. "For in Christ lives all the fullness of God in a human body,"[3] Jesus and I are walking this life hand in hand. Just like the testimony I shared in the previous pages, Jesus took my hand and said, "it would be like this from now on." The more air I breathe, the more this truth gets downloaded into me from this most loving statement he made to me. Today I receive the gift of trusting, Jesus. Trust in the Lord with all your heart; do not depend on your own understanding. Seek his will in all you do, and he will show you which path to take."[4]

God can use medicine to help us, but the focus is always on Jesus, who is my healer. If the enemy hadn't come at me through my health years ago, I most likely would have never chased after God so fervently. I most likely wouldn't be walking so closely with him now. "Desperate for more of Him" is what would accurately describe my constant state. It still is a valid description, but now the desperation is driven from a place of identity and love, not fear, knowing God and wanting him as my number one so desperately. Had I not walked in so much suffering, I most likely wouldn't be filled with such compassion for those who suffer.

Most often when I meet people today, my focus is on Jesus. Questions can arise inside me like, what do you want from him? Do you know

Him? Do you need a miracle? How can I pray for you? Now, when I pray for people at ministry events, church, the gym, the store, the airport or around the corner, I see God move. He shows up every time, and sometimes miracles happen right away. I am believing, the sometimes will turn into all the time. "Jesus looked at them intently and said, 'Humanly speaking, it is impossible. But not with God. Everything is possible with God."[5] There is such power in the name of Jesus. Life takes on a new flavor when your mortal existence is threatened. In my case, life was discovered and appreciated through every painful challenge.

GOD HAS THE FINAL SAY

Today, I choose to believe the truth. God is the final say. I believe whole-heartedly that every lying symptom of MS will be a thing of the past. If I lived a life letting my feelings guide me, I would never have been able to accomplish a tenth of what God has put before me. Feelings can lie to us. Faith has nothing to do with our feelings. It doesn't mean that I ignore what's happening. Denial is no way to live. There are actions God leads me to take concerning all areas of my everyday life.

Choosing to believe what God says and walking it out is different for us all. For me, it is hearing and believing what the Word of God and Holy Spirit says and then taking action when and where He says. "But don't just listen to God's word. You must do what it says."[6] Partnering with God and being obedient to Him by living the word only deepens my relationship with him. I try and keep it as simple as possible today. Over-thinking and complicating matters is in the past now, at least that's my hope. Surrendering my life to God and trusting Him, resting in him, he leads me. What a grand way, my only way, to do life.

A TRUE GIFT

Most of my encounters with the truth have happened in my daily life. I do love going to church and spending time with other believers worshipping God and hearing an anointed message. I am in relationship with Jesus; he is with me all the time. Yet, some of my most profound experiences with the Lord have happened in my car, my home, or living day to day. One of the oddest special places I have encountered the Lord is in my bathroom. He gets my attention there pretty regularly. I have seen bright lights moving very fast, which I believe were angels. I have heard from him, he gives me scripture, been touched by his healing power, his love and so much more, all in my bathroom. That's always a great way to start and end the day. All these beautiful supernatural experiences are beyond my human understanding. Walking with the Lord is more than these unexplainable experiences. I have been blessed to have character building, obedience, and much more.

MESSAGE OF OBEDIENCE

Obedience—a most common word we have all heard before. How is obedience defined? Webster describes it as; "an act, or instance in obeying." Sounds pretty clear, right? Taking it a step farther, here are a couple of illustrations of it in God's Word: "And this is love, that we walk according to his commandments; this is the commandment, just as you have heard from the beginning, so that you should walk in it."[7] Another word on obedience is "Blessed rather are those who hear the word of God and keep it!"[8] Living the word brings meaning to life. Obedience was about to take on new life one evening around ten pm, as I was driving home.

On my drive home one cool and clear Arizona fall night, I approached a red light. I saw a "smart car" tailgating a very large police SUV. I was now laughing out loud by myself in my auto. I love to laugh, and I like to think I have a good sense of humor. We were the only visible three cars on the roadway. Being my silly self, I was about to take a picture of this and put a playful post on Facebook. That's when it happened. As I was about to speak a funny post into my phone at the red light, my phone spelled out on its own, "There is a man up ahead, will you help him?" At first, I was baffled and a bit disturbed by this. My first thought was, how on earth does someone hack a smart phone?

I immediately erased the words off my phone. As I sat at the red light, I saw a man in my mind at the freeway exit asking for money. I then sensed Holy Spirit telling me to give him all the money I had in my wallet. It wasn't much, ten dollars. I said, out loud, "Is that you Lord?" By now, I had heard from the Lord many times. His Spirit and voice was becoming so clear to me. It was time to continue to drive, the green light indicated that. I approached my first of two freeways on my drive home. The first light was an entrance onto the freeway. As I sat at that red light, I looked around, and saw no one. It was a quiet night. There was an anticipation building, but I had no idea what to make of it.

All I could think as I traveled another five or so miles to the last freeway was, "Was that you Lord?" As I got off the last freeway before I got home, I approached another red light. I was the second car from the red light with one person behind me. My attention was pulled to a man up ahead standing on my left by the freeway exit who was holding a sign asking for help. The anointing was so powerful, it overtook me. I locked eyes with him and motioned to him with my hand to come over to my car. He then walked over with a beautiful smile. I told him out right, "the Lord told me you would be here, and he wanted me to give you this." He looked at me and smiled with such love in his eyes. He said so softly, "that's how it's done."

The light turned green, and I had to go because there were cars behind me. I was wrecked, and I burst into tears as I drove away. I thought, my God, what was that? What just happened? Immediately, I looked in my rearview mirror to see him one last time, and there was no sign of him anywhere. I said, "Lord was that an angel?" By the time I got home, five minutes later, God's presence was still so strong. I remember sitting in my home, thanking God for the encounter. That night, I went to sleep feeling so blessed by God.

When I awoke the next day, I had a whole new take on my experience the night before. Yes, I am so grateful, that may have been an angel encounter. Yet, what spoke the loudest was obedience, to hear from the Lord and simply obey his will. In that moment, I learned new dimensions of the gift of obedience. The encounter not only taught me how to simply obey, but that when we enter into the basics of obeying what his word says and what he shares with us intimately, it deepens our relationship with him. I believe It was training for hearing him and obeying. He has used me many places along the journey so far. It's usually not about Rachel. It's mostly about someone else. When I live my life surrendered to Him and His will, the roots of my existence only sink deeper into who I am, a daughter of God.

Every day when I awake, the journey has just begun. With eager anticipation, it's a fresh start every day, "and his mercies are new every morning."[9] If I didn't live the scripture below, I don't know if I would even be able to write this book. Allow me to share a little bit more what it looks like to walk the word out through a few of my life's challenges and opportunities.

LIVING FROM THE RIGHT TREE

A big part of it is a daily renewing of my mind that gives me the gift of a deeper intimacy with God. The word says it so well, "Don't copy the behavior and customs of this world, but let God transform you into a new person by changing the way you think. Then you will learn to know God's will for you, which is good and pleasing and perfect."[10] He is transforming me daily into more of the image of Christ. What does that mean? I look to the fruit of the Spirit. "But the Holy Spirit produces this kind of fruit in our lives: love, joy, peace, patience, kindness, goodness, faithfulness, gentleness, and self-control. There is no law against these things."[11] More miracles happened. I can honestly say I see evidence of the fruit of the spirit in my life today.

WHEN PAIN IS PRESENT

His peace fills me, especially during difficult time, be it a physical challenge, a heart break, a financial challenge, or any other circumstance. Today, I look to the Lord for everything, because he is where my help comes from. Each day is an opportunity to trust him more and more. One instance is fresh, and it comes to mind so clearly. Recently, my heart was hurt. I sought the Lord every day on my face for healing from the hurt. He gave me clear direction on how to walk in each day as he healed the hurts in my soul. Each day, I could sense his love for me. I actually fell more in love with Jesus during this trying time. He would encourage me in his word, saying, "he has a future and a hope for me."[12]

I also had wonderful mentors and friends helping me too. During this season, I was still able to be kind to others, not taking my hurts out on those around me. Most of whom I encountered had no idea what I was facing. It was still a joy to help someone in the midst of pain. My faith only grew during this time. Faith muscles were taking on a whole new form. My eyes are fixed on the Lord and the walk He has for me, and my hope comes from the Lord. Now, if this heart hurt had happened eleven plus years ago, my reactions and responses most likely would have been completely contrary to what I just shared.

Back then, I was still trying to control my life and others. I hadn't submitted to our loving God yet. I most likely would have blamed this person for hurting me. I may have said unkind things about him and to him. I might have been impatient and tried to force communication. Instead, I walk with the Lord now. Giving this person back to the Lord,

I told Jesus, I trust you, walking in forgiveness for him and myself. I didn't speak or think unkind things about this person or to anyone. I didn't pursue or contact the person, either. I let him go, blessed him, and moved on with Jesus. The revelation that I was a new creation and Jesus was all I needed took on new meaning during this time.

The deeper I went into trusting the Lord, the more I was able to receive how much he loved me. The power of God in my life is so very present today. This is an example of what it looks like when we submit our lives to Him. He is a much better steward of my life than I am. The realities of the truth in the word becomes so real to me during both challenging and good times now. Walking the word and reading it are two very distinct realities. For example, when we fully grasp the reality that we don't wrestle against flesh and blood, the veil is torn open. "For we are not fighting against flesh-and-blood enemies, but against evil rulers and authorities of the unseen world, against mighty powers in this dark world, and against evil spirits in the heavenly places."[13] We can see who the enemy really is. It really helps to not take the bait, which can come disguised as an offense.

LAYERS OF TRUTH REVEALED

Walking in the truth, I now know so much of what use to plague my thoughts, including the unloving or unkind acts of others, wasn't even about other people. I now know most of the time when it was negative or harmful, it was the flesh or an ungodly spirit operating. That truth makes forgiveness and walking in love so much more tangible. When I started to grasp this truth, a veil was torn open. My life is literally not my own. The reality of this becomes clearer with every encounter every day.

"This means that anyone who belongs to Christ has become a new person. The old life is gone; a new life has begun."[14] A new person? That is a daily discovery. I have been walking with the Lord for several years now, and this truth is just now being unveiled, daily. His Spirt now lives in me. Basically, when I invited Jesus into my heart and received Holy Spirit, I became who I was intended to be all along. With each breath, it is revealed, I am nothing without our living God—he is my everything. This is the best journey you could ever imagine.

My new nature is hopefully walking in the word with Holy Spirit. From airports, to the gym to South Africa, local restaurants, England, Romania, my work place, the grocery store, to the gas station, God has used me, simply because I said yes to him. I love to share His goodness with all whom I come into contact with. When we give Him our yes, we partner with Him, and that's when your adventure can take on new life like mine has. I have suffered much in my physical body through heartache and trauma. One thing remains the same, God is a good God, he never changes. He is the same yesterday, today, and forever.

God wrote my story, and I am just being obedient to write it down and share it. Perhaps you could say, I documenting what he did and does in my life, to show how powerful he is, how he loves us, how he heals, how he delivers, how he is with us through it all. God gets all the glory. He is the one who delivered me from so much. He is the one who healed my soul, my heart, and my body, and continues to do his work in me.

FROM A WITCH TO A SPIRIT-FILLED BELIEVER

Transforming from being a practicing witch to a Holy Spirit-filled Christian is a miracle only God can do. Changing from someone who had no idea who God was to walking with him hand in hand is a miracle only God can provide. Drugs and alcohol were filling God-shaped holes in my soul that only God was able to fill. Nineteen years of sobriety is certainly, a miracle only God can do. Going from knocking on death's door from

MS to suddenly experiencing a miracle in my body, is definitely a miracle only God can do. A life filled with fear and torment is now one of peace, love and comfort, another miracle only God can do. We have a miracle-working God, and the pages of this book attempt to illustrate this truth through my story in black and white.

WHAT WOULD YOUNGER RACHEL SAY?

If I was to talk to the myself before I knew Jesus, I wonder what I would say, to the Rachel I shared about in the beginning of the book? What would I say to the Rachel before she knew Jesus is the son of God; the Rachel who suffered from so much from tormenting spirits, before her life would change forever when she met Jesus face to face? I would most likely tell her my story if she wanted to listen.

I would tell her how free and loved she will be, and that she will have the most incredible life filled with hope and purpose. I would share how God is real and Jesus really saved her soul. She will never be the same after she receives Jesus as her Lord and Savior and life is about to get really good. I would tell the Rachel before she knew Jesus, how loved she is. It's a story I couldn't have written. I like to say, God wrote my story, and I am just writing it down.

Why? Why do I share this story? What was my purpose? A possible question arose through the pages. This word comes to mind, the word that Holy Spirit gave me the night I was told I had MS: "You're going to be just fine, Rachel, this isn't even about you." This truth sings the song I am trying to sing here in these pages, "And they have defeated him by the blood of the Lamb and by their testimony."[15] It is my heart to help others to know where to turn when they are in need. God is here for us all. Jesus is not a figure in the Bible. He is alive. When I met with him face to face life has never been the same. He is living truth. He is the son of God. He is the only way to Father God.

God has been with me my whole life, before I knew he existed right up until right now. This I know now. He is so much greater than anything this world has thrown at me.

IT HAS ONLY BEGUN

My journey from before I knew God existed until now has taken many turns. Yet, the great adventure is living this life hand in hand with Jesus. Gratitude for him takes on new meaning every day. This is an intimate adventure we all have been invited on. Imagine that, the son of God wants to be in a relationship with us all, intimately and personally. All we have to do is say yes. Yes, Jesus, I am a sinner, I confess that. Yes, Jesus, I believe you died so I can have a life. Wow! You're listening to me as I talk to you right now. Yes, Jesus, I want to say, "I am sorry for my sins, I choose to turn from my sins. Yes, Jesus, I invite you to live in my heart. Please come inside and make yourself at home in me. Take control of me. Fill me now with your Holy Spirit, who shows us how to live for you. My life is now yours." It's that simple.

The journey is different for us all, but one thing remains true. When you seek forgiveness from God, confess and believe that Jesus is Lord and be filled with the Holy Spirit, you're now a new creation. "This means that anyone who belongs to Christ has become a new person. The old life is gone; a new life has begun!"[16]

Picking up the word of God in the Bible is a great place to start, and getting plugged into a local church is a good suggestion, and a gift as well. When I started to go to church, that's where I experienced fellowship with other believers who wanted so much more of God too. They helped me, discipled me, and loved me. Wonderful loving people walked with me, helping me on my journey. Freedom and life was birthed the day I gave my life to Jesus. The old me was gone, and now, each day I discover the new me as I walk this road hand in hand with Jesus. We go from glory to glory as we are changed into his glorious image.

Going from death to life is literally my story. Before I encountered and received Jesus, I was living in sin, barely existing and not living yet. Today, I live and his Spirit lives in me. Jesus made it clear here, what it means to walk with him. "Jesus spoke to the people once more and said, "I am the light of the world. If you follow me, you won't have to walk in darkness, because you will have the light that leads to life."[17]

I know now he adopted me and chose me for his family. Ephesians 1:4-5 says, "Even before he made the world, God loved us and chose us in Christ to be holy and without fault in his eyes. God decided in advance to adopt us into his own family by bringing us to himself through Jesus Christ. This is what he wanted to do, and it gave him great pleasure." He chose me, he adopted me into his family, all through Jesus.

The revelation that life sprang forth in me the moment I met Jesus at twenty-one, is an undeniable truth. Jesus really is the son of God. Today, I know that I have life, I have Jesus. 1 John 5:11 "And this is what God has testified: He has given us eternal life, and this life is in his Son." When I received him as my Lord and Savior, and was filled with the Holy Spirit a couple years later, I literally became a new creation. Life is eternal with Jesus. John 17:3 says, "And this is the way to have eternal life—to know you, the only true God, and Jesus Christ, the one you sent to earth."

Since I have been walking with the Lord, all the trials, tribulations, battles, joy-filled moments, happy and sad moments have all been filled with life. It only brings me closer to Jesus. With God, all things are possible. Jesus is not only my savior, he's my best friend, my healer, and my deliverer. Life is unimaginable any other way. John 3:16 states, "For this is how God loved the world: He gave his one and only Son, so that everyone who believes in him will not perish but have eternal life. It's a journey we are all invited on. A journey I could never have imagined on my own with our loving God through Jesus Christ.

ENDNOTES

1. Mark 16:18
2. Luke 19:10
3. Colossians 2:9
4. Proverbs 3:5-6
5. Mark 10:27
6. James 1:22
7. 2 John 1:6
8. Luke 11:28
9. Lamentations 3:23
10. Romans 12:2
11. Galatians 5:22-23
12. Jeremiah 29:1
13. Ephesians 6:12
14. 2 Corinthians 5:17
15. Revelation 12:11
16. 2 Corinthians 5:17
17. John 8:12

CONCLUSION

Thank you for walking with me through pages of this book. The old has gone away, and the new is here now, because I invited Jesus into my heart. It was really that simple. Excitement fills me for what is next. A lot of my story I share here encompasses my discovery and experiences with our living God. It is my prayer that all who read the is book receive what God has for them. When I was searching for God, I remember hanging onto stories that talked about God and hope. Now, I can honestly and most confidently share, God defines my journey with him. Personal experiences with Jesus, Holy Spirit, and the Word have brought forth many life changing moments. I have hope in tomorrow, and hope in the plans and purposes God has for me. My story doesn't end here, because every day is new with our amazing God.

MEET THE AUTHOR

Rachel Benson's passion is to help people out of pain physically and spiritually. She loves to pray for people at the local grocery store, her church, and around the world. She has not only witnessed healing in her own life, but in the lives of countless others through prayer.

Part of her physical ministry is as a Licensed Massage Therapist in Arizona where she practices therapeutic massage. She holds a certificate of completion from the School of Kingdom Purpose located in Phoenix, Arizona, and is an ordained minister with Joan Hunter Ministries.

Rachel loves to travel and has been able to visit Romania, England and South Africa on ministry trips. Rachel desires to continue traveling the world, praying for the sick and sharing her miraculous testimonies.

Jesus has healed her heart, her mind and her body on countless occasions. Her journey with the Lord has been one filled with the miraculous, and now, miracles are the norm both in her life, and the many lives she's blessed to encounter.

www.RachelBenson.com

WORKS CITED

New Living Translation. Biblica, 2011. *BibleGateway.com,*

www.biblegateway.com/versions/NewLivingTranslation-NLT-Bible/#booklist

"Obedience." *Webster's Third New International Dictionary, Unabridged,*

Merriam-Webster, Inc., 2002. *Merriam-Webster.com,* https://www.merriam-webster.com/dictionary/obedience. Accessed 25 July 2017.

www.ingramcontent.com/pod-product-compliance
Lightning Source LLC
Chambersburg PA
CBHW071137090426
42736CB00012B/2141